The Person in the Chair

Becoming Your Authentic Self

James Protin

Foreword by Olivia DeRose Behanna

Aurora Corialis Publishing

Pittsburgh, PA

The Person in the Chair: Becoming Your Authentic Self

Paperback ISBN: 978-1-958481-00-4

Ebook ISBN: 978-1-958481-01-1

Printed in the United States of America

Cover by Karen Captline, BetterBe Creative

Developmental editing by Cori Wamsley

Copy editing by Renée Picard, Aurora Corialis Publishing

ADVANCE PRAISE

"People have come into my life; some have stayed and some have left. I truly believe that people are brought into your life at a specific time for a purpose. In *The Person in the Chair*, James tells his story through those people and challenges us to sit in the chair for both our own self-discovery and to help others with their life goals. Live, Love, Learn, Pray, and Inspire are not only words to live by but a basis for personal growth. James shows us by example how to live the words and make a difference in this world. This book is for those looking to find their way and those who shine the light."

~ Diane Altland

———

"*The Person in the Chair* is real, raw, and pure inspiration! This book gives a fresh and beautiful perspective about how we navigate through life and learn from its continuous mountains and valleys.

"Jim's personal stories and life lessons are written in such a way that readers can relate to them from their own experiences. I guarantee this book will leave you feeling inspired about your future and filled with hope not only for your own life, but for those around you who you love. You will leave the book a better person than when you entered!"

~ Melissa Migliaro

———

"In a time where we insist on curating our perceived image, this book rips off the Band-Aid exposing the core of every human. When accountability thrives, and blame is extinguished, we rise, and authenticity becomes the standard. Without the filters, we are free to engage in relationships that keep us in a constant state of transformation. This is a powerful challenge to embrace your own legacy to make an impact."

~ Lynn Berry

————

"A wonderful read, where James Protin provides not a road map, but a set of his own footprints to follow in life's journey. This book is more than a typical self help guide, as it is written with truth, honesty, an open heart, and an earnest willingness to share James's personal story.

"The reader will find that they are exactly where they have chosen to be, and that they possess the power to overcome adversities and change their lives. James is there for the reader who feels alone, who needs to learn about the five pillars, and who wants to absolutely change their future for the good. James will sit in the reader's chair while telling his story."

~ Rory Gazdick

TABLE OF CONTENTS

FOREWORD

By Olivia DeRose Behanna

Life has a mysterious way of creating our journeys. In my case, the journey was filled with joy and despair, happiness and sorrow, life and (almost) death all before the age of five.

Although this journey was mine, I never faced it alone.

My parents are the greatest people I have ever known. My dad could do anything you could think of. He worked for a technology company during the first few years of my life. He was the goofiest man in the whole wide world. My mom is a funeral director in our hometown. She is the kind of woman that you knew exactly how she felt with just a look. She helped other people during the hardest time in their life; it was her superpower to pick up the pieces.

My sisters are everything to me. They are my biggest headaches, but my most fierce supporters. Growing up with all sorts of girl power surrounding me was incredible. We had everything because we had each other, and nothing could get in our way.

Life was crazy, but it was normal for us.

Well, that was the truth for about four years—then we heard the three words that would change our world forever.

"She has cancer."

The Person in the Chair

When I sat down to write this, I knew that I wanted to write it right. Although, I found it more difficult to put the story on paper. There were so many different things that happened regarding cancer in my life that capturing the entire story in a few short pages would be challenging. So, with a plethora of memories and some grace from God, I'll start the story at the beginning.

I often wondered how people learned they were sick. Perhaps a doctor's visit or abnormal pain. For me, it was my dad. My dad found the tumor. I know that sounds absurd but it's true. He was helping me dry off after a bath when he noticed that my stomach was hard. He could feel a huge mass on the left side of my body.

After being examined by my worried parents, they called the doctor. I had some tests done the very next day. The doctor told my parents that I had a softball-sized Wilms' Tumor, or a nephroblastoma, on my kidney and that I would require further testing from doctors at the Children's Hospital of Pittsburgh. I don't think anyone knew what this discovery would mean for me and my family, but we would soon find out.

Six days later, the doctors had the results. Not only was this tumor cancerous, but it was already in stage IV and had metastasized into my lungs. I went into surgery the next day, but the tumor was too big to remove. Our game plan had changed and now included chemotherapy and radiation. I underwent treatments for six weeks before it was safe to remove the tumor. I had a port near my armpit to help administer fluids and draw blood.

I was desperately afraid of needles; needless to say, this was a very long six weeks! Afterward, not only did they take the tumor out, but also my entire left kidney.

A question that I get a lot is, "do you remember any of it?" The short answer is yes. I remember a lot of different, random things. It's like a movie with flashbacks when I think about what happened. I remember putting on blush and pink lipstick in the bathroom after my hair was cut short. I remember eating bowls of kiwi at midnight before the tests that required fasting. I remember sitting in my hospital bed while my mom ate pretzels in the chair next to me. I remember a bookshelf full of Disney VHS tapes, specifically *Snow White and the Seven Dwarves*, and a computer room on my floor [of the hospital] where I played a Harry Potter game.

I remember walking down the hall still connected to all my IVs. I remember getting stuck six times with a needle during a CT scan but getting a Cinderella Barbie doll after making it through. I remember the giant door closing in the radiation room while I laid perfectly still on a cold table with lasers hitting me; the way my throat hurt after all the treatments; the numbing cream they put over my port before needing my blood drawn; bringing my angel doll, Heavenly Angel, into the tests with me and getting her a hospital bracelet, too.

I recall a stuffed white dog that held my oxygen in my hospital bed and drinking a nasty-flavored drink in Styrofoam cups in the waiting room before testing.

I woke up in the hospital with a giant Band-Aid over my scar, which needed to be removed. My doctor's jokes covered the sting from his cold hands as he examined my abdomen. When I was finally home, I sat on my living room floor opening gifts my classmates had sent me. Most profoundly, I remember receiving the sacrament of Anointing of the Sick in the rectory of my church and being told, "I'm praying for you" by almost everyone we knew.

It's a strange thing to process when you're so young, even now as an adult.

By the age of five, I had one kidney, two very noticeable scars, and enough hospital visits under my belt to last a lifetime. Not many kids can say this, but I was also a preschool dropout. The early years of my life were pretty rough for my family. I can't imagine what it was like for them to watch their daughter and sister go through all of this as a child. My parents, grandparents, sisters, aunts, and uncles watched me endure hardships that no one should ever have to go through. My little sister spent a lot of time without my parents during her own childhood, because they were so occupied with my diagnosis and securing my health. It was a time in life that wasn't fair to anyone.

Cancer is an extremely difficult thing to deal with, irrespective of age, for the person going through it and their caregivers. Looking back over the years, I realized that cancer continued to destroy things in my life.

For several years, I still didn't have much hair. I looked like a boy up until about second grade. My mom often recalls a moment with me and another child when they asked me why I wore headbands if I didn't have any hair. My answer? Because it matches my outfit, obviously!

Living without my hair was weird, and I never quite felt like myself without long hair. A majority of my childhood photos are of me with barely any hair. Learning to love yourself at that age wasn't really taught, so I just did what I knew and went on with the show. After high school, it seemed like every girl I knew chopped their hair off. It was the thing to do, I guess. But I never thought to myself, "I should do that, too." I remember walking in the lobby at college and a lifelong friend of mine I hadn't seen in a while said to me, "I knew that was you from a mile away; that long hair is your trademark."

At that moment, I knew that not only was it my trademark, but it was also my trophy. Struggling for years with hair issues is no joke. It breaks you down in ways you would never imagine. But this hair is a result of the battle I won, and I will wear it proudly as my triumphant crown for as long as I can... except now, it's sprinkled with gray.

As I grew up, I noticed that my body wasn't changing like all my friends. It was something I really didn't understand for a while. Not going through puberty like all my other girlfriends came with a lot of jealousy and confusion. I couldn't wear a lot of the same clothes without looking like a boy. Bras didn't fit me. Formal dresses didn't fit me. Getting away without altering a dance costume was a miracle. Not looking like everyone else, or even looking *normal* and *proportionate,* is still awkward to cope with. I think about getting married someday and how hard it might be to find a dress that fits right. This struggle has never really gone away. I'm still learning to love my body.

Dealing with my looks was one thing, but feeling inferior was another. This one started pretty young. I went to a private elementary school, so we went to our local YMCA for gym class. We played all kinds of sports and games there every Thursday... Well, everyone else did. I always remember hearing, "You have to be really careful because if you get hit in your kidney, it could be really bad." And so began the role of being the catcher. In any game we played, I had to be in whatever position could get hurt the least. Needless to say, I never got into sports.

All of these things seem a little juvenile when I think about how cancer has affected me mentally. There have been moments in my life where I feel like everything is surreal. I'm in love with the people I'm with, the places I'm at, and the things I'm doing. I'm happy with my career and all the work I have done to get me where I am. During moments like these, I seem to always thank God for giving me a second chance at life. If He had decided to call me home as a child, I would never have been granted opportunities, nor would I have been asked so graciously to craft the foreword to this incredible book. I would've never been able to perform in Disney World, graduate top of my class, meet my best friends, or have a job I love. Simply, the life I have is because God gave me a second chance.

However, with this feeling comes the polar opposite which normally comes to me in the form of a question: *Why did God let me live?* When you're on top of the world, this thought never crosses your mind. Unfortunately, there are periods of time when I cannot understand why God gave me a second chance. I've gone through things that feel like the end of the world to most people. Breakups, losing people I love, toxic situations, doing everything right and still feeling useless, differences of opinions that turn into cold wars.

Oftentimes, it's little things that make me question my survival. If my dad didn't find the cancer when he did, if I didn't get medical attention... then we would not be having *this* problem or *that* problem. I will be the first person to tell you that I can be a sensitive person who overthinks everything. It's a bizarre thing to think about from the outside looking in. People tend to think that I should always be grateful and ecstatic that I was cured. It's not that I am *not*; it's just that some days are harder than others.

Just like the physical hardships, this is something I am still learning to live with. I understand that my cancer has no bearing on the ups and downs God has in store for me... it's an easy thing to blame my problems on, my scapegoat. While it is something I don't think I'll ever completely grow out of, I'm working on healthier habits when life gets to be too much for me.

On the contrary, there are many good things that arose from this hardship. Shortly after I was diagnosed, I was recognized as a "Make-A-Wish kid." The Make-A-Wish Foundation is a nonprofit that grants wishes to children between 2.5 and 18 years old who are fighting critical illnesses. This five-year-old girl had a really important wish to make. I decided that my biggest wish was to meet the Disney Princesses. We worked with some truly amazing people who sent me and my family to Florida. My family was hosted by Give Kids the World Village where we could visit the Castle of Miracles, eat ice cream every morning for breakfast, and hang out with the coolest rabbit governor, Mayor Clayton.

I had a small star made with my name on it that a fairy placed on the ceiling of the castle while I was sleeping. I'll never forget the magic that the village provided for us. We still go back when we visit Florida to relive the memories we made there and to visit my old star.

Meeting the Princesses was one of the most magical times in my entire life. To this day, I am the biggest Disney fan and will bawl my eyes out when I see the Princesses in Walt Disney World. When we went to the parks, I got to wear a Make-A-Wish pin that indicated to cast members that I could skip the line. I will always remember meeting the characters and how kind they were to my family. Their faces are imprinted on my memory and their compassion on my heart. Witnessing the characters with any child is magical, but there is something special when you know that child is suffering. When people know a child needs healing, magic is seen in so many ways.

People did a number of things for us at home that made us feel extremely loved. I remember having a spaghetti dinner fundraiser to help with treatment expenses. A lot of my memories stem from photos of my family at this event. My community also put together an event called Overcoming Obstacles for Olivia. There were bouncy houses (that I was broken-hearted that I couldn't play in), clowns doing tricks, princesses posing with children for photos, games, entertainment, and raffles. I remember being so shy and nervous there that I held my mom's hand the whole time.

My older sister and all her closest friends came and took princess photos with me. It is truly a blessing when a community comes together for a good cause. I am still so grateful for my community and all they did for me and my family during our time of need.

Last year, I stumbled across a newspaper article that was written about me—"Dance to aid ailing Carroll Township Girl," by Stacy Wolford. I can't read it without crying. It begins with a quote from my baby sister, "We tell the angels to make Olivia's belly better." My little sister, only three years old, was asking the angels to help me. I know it wasn't easy to understand, but it helped me realize how much my family cared... how much everyone cared. The article mentions that my family was receiving cards and money from people we had never even met. It leaves me completely speechless. It makes the days when I feel so alone a little easier.

People who knew me as a young girl still ask me how I'm doing to this day. They'll say reluctantly, "Were you the one who was sick?" When I confirm that it was me, they tell me how they prayed for me. A lot of these amazing people are ones I barely remember. I cannot describe the blessing that is my community.

My experience with cancer has given me a voice that I now use in ways I never would have dreamed of before, and I use it to inform and inspire others. I have told my story in front of hundreds of people at Relay for Life several times, at churches, and at dance recitals. Discussing my experience is always on the table, and I'm willing to share it with anyone who asks. It's not scary or upsetting to talk about... it's my life.

To you, it might be a taboo topic to discuss openly, but please know that, to me, it's just another part of my journey. If you're reading this and want to know more, don't hesitate to talk to me about it.

The beauty that has come out of my journey is that I get to connect with others. I have been able to tell my story to hundreds of people at a time, but I have also been able to have one-on-one conversations. People have reached out to me on social media to ask for advice or inspiration when their children were sick. I think the one thing that people want to hear about is what the experience of going through something this traumatic is like and how it affects a person's life.

People have a hard time listening to doctors or those in a clinical setting. I know how shocking it was to my parents to hear that I was sick. The diagnosis can come off as cold or nonchalant. But talking to someone who knows what it is like to be sick or someone who knows how to be a caregiver can be, in a way, comforting. Being open about my experience with cancer has brought many friendships into my life.

When I was in high school, I performed a solo in my annual dance recital to "I'm Gonna Love You Through It" by Martina McBride. We called it my "cancer dance." My mom and I adorned my costume with a cancer ribbon covered in crystals. For the recital, I wanted to do something special, so I recorded a short speech telling my story to be played before I started dancing. I stood with my back to the audience while they listened to my experience with cancer. I explained how I was unable to dance in the recital when I found out I was diagnosed, but how grateful I was to stand on the stage again and dance. I received a standing ovation that night.

After the recital, I was approached by a man I had never met, James Protin. We took a photo together and exchanged some words about my journey, and he commended my strength. He became a friend to me and my family. We connected through social media and ran into each other at events over the years. He always made it clear that I had a gift... that everyone has a gift. Mr. Protin always encouraged me to tell my story, to be myself, and to speak from my heart. I never would have thought that years later, I would be writing the foreword to his book. A book filled with a lifetime of experiences with the same core themes as mine. A book that will be an inspiration to others on this crazy journey we call life.

I'm not sick anymore like I used to be. I go to the hospital once a year for different tests and see a special team of doctors and researchers. I am actually a part of the Survivorship Clinic at the Children's Hospital of Pittsburgh where they will study my body to see the long-term effects of my treatments. They will see me until I'm 26 years old.

That year is coming pretty quickly, and it makes me cry when I think about it. My nurses and doctors have been such a huge, influential part of my life. Navigating life without them is something I haven't done yet. They are some of my biggest fans and are always so supportive of everything I do.

I truly will never be able to thank them enough for saving my life. Dr. Wollman, Dr. Tersak, Nurse Rose, and Nurse Autumn, thank you from the bottom of my heart. I am grateful to you, God, and everyone who has been by my side along the way.

Moving forward, I find it important to mention what I have learned. First and foremost, I have learned that family and friendship are the absolute most important things in the entire world. You truly never know when God will call you home, so let your loved ones know how much they mean to you. When I was small, my mom would say, "Hug me like you mean it. This could be the last time you ever see me." As I grew up, I made it a point to make known how much I loved my family and friends.

Second, spend time with yourself and love yourself. You are different from any other person in the entire world. There is no one else quite like you, and that in itself is special. Love yourself and use your strengths for good. Remember that you create your world, so fill it with magic.

Third, know that you are a light in the world. You have brightened someone's life without even knowing it. Like Mr. Protin told me, *you* have a gift. You were born with gifts and talents. The older you get, the more opportunities you have to share them with the world.

Normally I end my speeches about my journey with the quote, "They say 'what doesn't kill you makes you stronger,' and for me, cancer did just that." This time, I want to emphasize that every person has a different journey, but we all have a voice. We all have different messages to share with the world. The message I share is one of hope, love, encouragement, and faith. Your journey may offer a similar or drastically different message than mine. However, we each have our own voice.

How we decide to share our voice with the world is up to us. I will continue to share mine with the world, and I hope you do, too.

Keep going. I love you all.

INTRODUCTION

You see, what happened was... wait, I'm going to stop right there.

Let me be perfectly clear: I'm not looking for sympathy or pity in writing this book. I'm not a victim; in fact, I've caused more pain than I've endured. You won't find a single excuse or explanation. I'm a flawed human being on a journey of personal transformation—from the dark depths of depression, through the chaos of anxiety brought on by an ego that bordered on narcissism. I'm the arsonist who created a perfect storm that burned my life to the ground.

I own all of it.

If you have never woken up unable to look in the mirror because you loathe everything about yourself, you likely won't understand my story. But I hope you continue reading because you might learn something about your fellow humans. If it seems like that scenario is playing out for you through too many mornings to count, I hope the lessons I share in the pages ahead help you to heal.

I want nothing more than for you to experience the good stuff life has in store for you.

I have spent nearly 20 years becoming. In that time spent seeking a better understanding of who I am, some moments have left an indelible mark on my heart, and I'll admit, some of them sting to this day. But for us to heal from anything, we have to feel it. We can't simply ignore it until it goes away.

That's the difference between acceptance and surrender. Acceptance is seeing who you are, feeling your truth, then showing up every day loving the skin you're in...with all its flaws. When you hide from who you are, deny your truth, and try to become someone you're not ... that's surrendering to pressure from a society that desperately wants you to settle for being a face in the crowd.

We all have flaws. We all make mistakes. Accepting and embracing the life we're given makes us whole. Once you've accepted and love who you are, nothing will offend you, and no one can ever use your flaws against you. For a while, I really believed that life had gotten the best of me, until I understood that every experience was sent to make me a better human.

Accepting myself as I am, started me on the path to embracing anything and everything life threw at me, and allowed me to learn from it.

My journey, the one my heart is guiding me along, started many years ago now. I'm still here, walking forward, the bag on my shoulder carrying gratitude, humility, vulnerability, love, and grace. It's been a rollercoaster ride, slowly climbing each hill, then speeding down the other side a little out of control, with a lot of twists and turns thrown in along the way.

Maybe that's why I don't like rollercoasters.

Am I proud of my life journey? No ... but I'm not ashamed either. It's my story, written by my own hand. I won't hide from it. I let my heart feel it. It has allowed me to grow into my flaws and has made me who I am today. The obstacles I encountered made me physically capable as a young man. As the miles added up, my physical abilities have naturally diminished a bit. But I'm stronger today than I have been at any other time in my life, because I'm also emotionally and spiritually capable.

The adversity that has accompanied me on my journey has taught me how to control my emotions and nurture my soul. That growth has led me to live my life in physical, emotional, and spiritual alignment. It hasn't made me better than anyone else; it has only made me better than who I was yesterday and prepared me to become better than I am today. These pages contain a compilation of lessons learned along my personal journey of rebirth from the devastation of a life lost ... my own. My journey has been humbling in many ways, and this book is my heart's eyewitness account of that journey.

It will be a bit raw at times, but I promise you one thing: from here through to the very last page, it is honest.

Being alone with myself and a blank page is one of the scariest things I've ever done. I think that's why I love it. Some time ago, a mentor of mine suggested I start journaling, and it's been one of the best things I've ever done.

It's helped me get to know myself.

That may sound strange, but when you think about it ... do you really know yourself? We are all so busy that we often don't.

When I stare at a blank page and my heart comes unlocked and I spill my insides all over the page, what comes out is brutally honest, sometimes painful, and always enlightening.

With all your senses open ... the truth has a way of leaking out.

And when you know yourself deeply, you become that person, the one staring back at you from the page. Not the one that you "should" be.

Until I started journaling, I didn't realize that I wasn't being open and honest with myself. And if I'm not open and honest with myself, how could the people around me see my joys and my struggles? The real stuff? I kept it hidden. I was stuffing it down and putting on a mask so others wouldn't judge me, but they also couldn't see ME, the real me. And that was what held me back from not only being the person I wanted to be but also connecting with people on a deep level, authentically.

It took a long time for me to care more about what *I* think of me than what others think of me. It's hard. We become so concerned with the perception of others, that we lose sight of who we really are.

The truth in my heart has led me to beautiful people and amazing places. It let me stop being afraid to spill my guts on the page. It opened the door to really living.

Before that though ... I felt lost, alone, and completely empty inside. I showed up for everything and everyone ... everywhere. But I wasn't showing up for myself. All this showing up was what I was *supposed* to do, not what I wanted to do. I wasn't showing up present and available in the full capacity of who I am.

But my life looked really good on paper, right?

- ✓ Great job
- ✓ Beautiful family
- ✓ Comfortable home, nice car
- ✓ Giving back to the community

Inside though, I was sad, depressed, and hopeless (check, check, check).

Ultimately, we all will be held accountable to who we are inside. We don't live our lives on paper.

Making the change from who you are to who you are meant to be isn't easy. To this day, there is a constant struggle between who I was and who I am becoming. There is nothing keeping you tethered to where you are. You have to make a choice to discover your true self, align with your values, and become what I like to call a "lighthouse:" a beacon for others on the same journey to gather, get support, and rise together.

Sure, it can seem impossible when you're lost on the ocean of all the "shoulds," all the checklists, all the "supposed-tos" in your life.

Even Mt. Everest was once considered insurmountable. Sir Edmund Hillary proved that it *could* be conquered, though. Since then, over 4,000 people have reached the summit of earth's tallest peak.

I've always been fascinated by numbers, and 29,029 is my favorite number. It's the height in feet of the summit of Mt. Everest, the literal top of the world. When I was sitting at the bottom, figuratively, I knew I was meant for more. So, I climbed my way back. I cut through every excuse until I was left with nothing but the raw, unfiltered truth. And I'm still climbing.

The Empty Chair

From the time I was a kid, Doodles (my dad) always told me a story about a wonderful gift I received the day I was born. A chair.

The Person in the Chair

He said that on the day of our birth we all have an empty chair waiting for us. It's a chair that we will carry throughout our lives, from place to place, year after year. The chair will have a profound impact on our lives, not for its style but for its various occupants. The chair will be occupied by the people who will guide us emotionally, physically, and spiritually in our lives.

At first, the person occupying our chair is a parent, but throughout our lives, our person in the chair will change, continuously replaced by someone new. The person will sit in the chair for different reasons. Parents, grandparents, siblings, friends, teachers, and coaches will be in our chair.

I have been blessed to have great teachers in my life, people close to me as well as total strangers who have had an indelible impact on my life.

Of course, my father was the first to occupy my chair. He raised me to be a lifelong learner and to always strive to achieve my best. From him, I learned to believe there is something valuable to take away from every single person and thing we encounter along our journey. The most influential people in my life represent a broad spectrum of my life experience, for a wide variety of reasons, some good and some bad ... yes you can learn and grow from the negative people and experiences too. But, my father will always be far and away the biggest influence in my life.

Mark Twain said, "The two most important days in your life are the day you are born and the day you find out why." One morning I woke up, and something clicked. It didn't come naturally. I had to look in the mirror and confront the ugly image looking back at me. I had to slay the monster that had owned me for far too long. But in that moment, I finally knew *why*. That day I reached out to Doodles, and we had a serious conversation ... real talk. We revisited the empty chair story, and all the lessons of live, love, learn, pray, and inspire that I had suppressed, came rushing to the surface.

My "why" had been inside me all along, bubbling up toward the surface for decades, but one day in the summer of my fortieth year, it collided with my conscious mind, and I was confused, lost, and angry. I didn't feel like myself. I didn't know where I was supposed to go from that place. I looked externally for answers that didn't come.

Everybody I had loved turned away.

Doodles told me the first thing I had to do is to confront what I didn't want to confront. Tell the truth and take ownership ... and never relinquish it. When I finally learned the lesson, things began to shift.

It turns out that you need very little to make a happy life. Everything you will ever need is within yourself, in your way of thinking. Speaking the truth and living true to your word through your actions is the key to believing in the possible and living your best life. Don't wait for someone else to believe in you; believe in yourself. And forgive.

I'm new to forgiveness. Having spent much of the first half of my life neither giving nor receiving it in any form. Nobody put me there ... I did that on my own. I became an expert in self-loathing. I have been angry, resentful, and unforgiving ... the result of choices and decisions I take full responsibility for.

When I look at the amazing humans in my life, I find something I wasn't expecting. I am surrounded by humans who love, believe, and trust in the man I am and who know I'm here to do great things. Even when I don't see myself, I see the love around me.

Even when my chair is empty, I understand how to have faith in myself.

When it is empty, we may feel as though we have been cast off, not really knowing our destination. These are the defining times of our lives when we must draw from the lessons of its previous occupants.

At some point, you will be called upon to sit in someone's chair. When your time comes, take great care. You must never sit in someone's empty chair unless you plan to fill it, not just occupy it. To fill it is to do so with love, compassion, kindness, and a bit of discipline and hard work.

Once, a stranger told me the same story about the significance of a simple empty chair that is waiting for us on the day of our birth. At first, I thought this was random; at this point in my life, I had all but forgotten my father's chair talks. The man told me a teacher he admired told him the story of a chair that will have a profound impact on his life because of its various occupants, who guide us emotionally, physically, and spiritually. He smiled when he told me that the teacher was the most significant occupant of his chair, and even though many others have sat there over the years, the teacher remained.

He teared up when he told me that the teacher and that chair changed his life.

At a time when being different was a heavy burden to bear, the teacher sitting in his chair had lightened his load. In the dark time when his chair was empty, and he felt most alone, the teacher would come and sit in his chair. The lessons he learned from the teacher shaped who he would become, and he raised his sons in the same manner. One chair made generations of impact.

The stranger didn't know it, but that teacher was my father.

There is a reason I was in that place standing next to that man at that time. We were both meant to be there. We were meant to have that conversation, because at that moment, that conversation quite possibly saved my life. It pulled me back to that chair where my father taught me about Live, Love, Learn, Pray, and Inspire ... his five pillars.

We've all had at least one mentor, teacher, leader, friend, or parent who has sat in that chair and impacted our lives in some positive way. Someone who has made a difference in our lives, who has made us better, and helped us become the adults we are today. I've been blessed to have three.

That brings me to the second most important day of my life. On October 10, 1997, Terrilynn, who is now my wife, sat down in my chair and helped me understand why I was born. More on that later.

One look at Terrilynn, and you will immediately say, "Jamie, you out kicked your coverage." And I will quickly agree. She is the most beautiful woman I have ever known. She is intelligent, mildly funny—I am working on that—and has the kindest heart and sweetest soul you will ever find. Terrilynn also has an amazing ability: to see me for who I truly was, even when I didn't know myself who I was.

There was a time when I wouldn't describe myself as a good man. My ex-wife knew it. My children knew it. My boss knew it. Heck, even my dog knew it. But, thankfully Terrilynn saw something few, if any, others could see. She saw past the bumps and bruises, the sticky mess, and knew there was a good man. She brought him into her life, into her family, and she fell in love with him. And did she ever love that young fella. It caught him off guard.

Nobody had ever loved him like that.

When the young fella stumbled, she picked him up. When he strayed off the path, she showed him the way home. When he stood under the judgment of others, she stood with him. When the young fella was sitting on rock bottom, she sat with him. When the young fella started climbing, she held the ladder. When the young fella had his head in the clouds, she grounded him. When the young fella just could not see love, she showed him and the entire world what true love means. This woman held his hand and walked through the gates of hell. And she never even flinched.

There has been one other occupant of my chair. Perhaps not as significant as Doodles or Terrilynn, but just as important. He is the one responsible for the coffee stains and crumbs in the cushion: Bruce Fletcher, AKA "Swaggy B." He gave me the best job I ever had and set my feet on the path of a very successful career. To be honest, it has been a career that likely doesn't happen without him.

When I met him 20 years ago, I was still broken. I had already been working in the engineering industry for about 15 years and had really gone nowhere. But, Swaggy B saw something—who knows what, his mind works a bit differently than most, but he saw it.

I am very grateful that he did.

God puts the people we need in our lives, when we need them. Terrilynn and Swaggy B showed up right on cue, bringing exactly what I needed when I did not even know what I needed or what I'm actually here for. If not for them, and others who raised their hand and took their place in my chair ... my purpose would have remained lost in the fog of depression.

It's Time to Fill the Chair

Mentors come from all walks of life and show up when you least expect it. However, there is no more powerful and life-changing mentor who will occupy your chair than you. Yes, *you* sit in your own chair when you reflect back on the lessons of your life and learn from them. After all, what's the point of lessons if you don't learn and grow?

And when you aren't in your own chair, shine the brightest light possible for the youngsters who are next. That's how you fill a chair. Share your lessons. You can either learn by experiencing the lessons yourself or you can learn by listening, and as someone who has learned from a lot of bumps and bruises, I could have listened a little more and dealt with fewer scrapes.

The people who sat in my chair helped me grow immensely. And they inspired this book because I want *you* to be able to sit in someone's chair, especially your own. I also wanted to take a minute to sit in your chair and tell you about what I've discovered in my life to be the pillars of joy, living authentically, and being who you were meant to be.

The words written in the ensuing pages are from my heart. The concept of Live. Love. Learn. Pray. Inspire. is the foundation of the simple art of living an honorable life as taught to me by my father. These pillars, instilled in me as a child, and rediscovered in middle-age, motivated me to seek the inspiration

I needed to find balance in all things and live a full life. They are the foundation on which I have rebuilt my life. They guided me to my calling. They have become my ministry.

Live. Love. Learn. Pray. Inspire. Create a perfect alignment of mind, body, and spirit. Everything in life flows from these five pillars. When things go wrong and the storms rage, your life will become dark. If you are to weather the storm, meet the challenges, conquer the adversity, and rise, you must have a strong foundation.

The thing I learned from the adversity in my life, the thing that holds us back—the only thing—is our unwillingness to step forward. I know it's hard. I've learned all too painfully that it's supposed to be. Nothing worth doing is going to be easy. Some of us had to hit rock bottom and run out of excuses before I—I mean "we"—took that step.

This book is a collection of lessons learned, motivational thoughts, and stories culled from the good and bad experiences of my life so you can *feel* your way through life. Live in your heart, not in your head.

I want you to be the light in someone's darkness, to be the person in the chair, when they most need it. And I want to be the person in your chair when YOU most need it, through this book.

Dear 1976 Jamie,

Doodles was right ... about everything. You're going to learn as an adult what he had already taught you as a child. Of course, you're going to learn it the hard way ... years later. Because that's just who you are.

Don't worry, he knows this and is preparing you for your future adversity. You're going to step in some messes. Like I said, you can't help yourself. Your heart will break a few times. Your world will become dark, all will seem lost, you will be lost. You're going to grope around for a few years, but remember to be patient. You'll shine brighter on the other side.

Without you even knowing, he was building his boy into a good man. You learned your love of people, all people, from him. Your sense of humor, your kindness and empathy, your love of life, learning, teaching, and talking, grew from his example.

And don't lose sight of Saundra. Your work ethic comes from her. Those 60-hour weeks in your future will be easy because of her. Your mental toughness, that came from her. It will get you through some difficult times. You'll learn that you're more like her than you think.

Doodles knew he would be gone one day, and he made sure you were prepared. You're going to have deep conversations with him. None more important than the ones you'll have during the last three weeks of his life. Pay attention. Follow your heart or you'll spend the rest of your life wishing you had. Live your life with a sense of purpose and mission like he did.

Never forget, you will forever be his boy.

The Person in the Chair

Warmest regards,

2018 Jamie

Dear Reader: Try writing your own letter to your younger self ... you may be surprised what you read.

PART I
THE FIVE PILLARS OF LEADERSHIP

My father taught me the five pillars of leadership by example. Every time I sought advice, as he sat in my chair, he showed me the foundation for living a good life.

LIVE

"I've had a great life ... no regrets. But if I had one wish ... I'd ask for one more day with your mother."

~ Doodles

I am truly a blessed man. It doesn't matter if I lost yesterday. It doesn't matter if I had my heart broken yesterday. It doesn't matter. I woke up today. I'm alive ... having an amazing cup of coffee, waiting for a beautiful sunrise. I have yet another beautiful day, another chance to get it right.

I'm going all-in on life today. You with me? Today I will take nothing for granted. I'm going to be grateful, thankful, and appreciative. I'll smile and say "hello" to a stranger, hug the people I love, trust God to put me where He needs me, and write a new chapter of my story.

My life isn't perfect, I'm sure yours isn't either. We're imperfect humans living in an imperfect world. None of us asked to be on this journey, but since we are, let's make it the best we can.

"Live" is the first pillar because nothing else happens until you first choose to stand up and courageously live your life, rather than being battered by the waves and dragged wherever the undertow takes you.

When you wake up in the morning, you are alive. But being alive is a stationary circumstance. You are not truly living by merely existing. To live requires movement: physical, of course, but also mental and emotional. You must accept and acknowledge your dark, negative thoughts just as you embrace your vibrant, positive thoughts. Your feelings of sadness are equally as important as your feelings of joy.

What does it mean to live? Humans have been searching for the meaning of life for as long as there have been, well, humans. Life is a precious gift, and to live it is to honor the giver.

I see living as going about the business of being alive. To live means to feel your beating heart, knowing that it is much more than just a muscle and following it wherever it leads. It means breathing in all the laughter and smiles, touching and tasting every fear. It means seeing vividly between the lines and listening deeply to the deafening silence in your mind.

To live, you must understand *why* you are alive. Alive is a state of being ... a gift from God. Living is putting your gift into action and sharing it with the rest of the world. I started living when Terrilynn came into my life. She showed me that living is showing gratitude to God for His gift, and she lent me the courage to look at how I had selfishly squandered His blessing.

Life doles out its lessons in different ways. Some come to us gently, wrapping around our shoulders like a supportive parent. But some come to us like a shovel to the face. If we are truly blessed, our purpose comes to us gently. But for those of us ... like me ... who learn our lessons the hard way ... well, we get the shovel.

I took my gift for granted, because I was afraid to use it. To understand why this gift has been given to us, we must be brave enough to live. None of us is here for ourselves. We are here for each other. The path you have taken to where you are right now is not random; it has been a building block in the construction of you. Own all of it. Own your bumps and bruises, forgive the sins of the past, and allow yourself to be forgiven. Through our human connection, living our personal journey will create lessons that will change the world.

Without trying, without intention, we impact the lives of others every day. So why not invest more in each interaction than anyone would ever expect? Don't just go through the motions. Make the commitment to live. While others are making noise, be a caring, focused, generous human. Invest completely in the simple connection between humans. You will create empowerment, inspiration, love, and kindness, and change the trajectory of someone's life.

When I was a young man, I lived in the shallow end of the pond. Always splashing around making noise, but never getting under the surface of who I am. Allowing myself to be blissfully unaware of my life that was passing me by at an ever-increasing rate of speed.

I was always fascinated by change but hesitant to embrace it. Then when I was 40 years old, I decided to make the deep dive. It was a long way to the bottom, to authenticity, but when I got there, suddenly, I had substance. I started writing and making connections. Since then, I've met Jamie Protin, and I like him. I like his awareness and his desire to continuously better himself.

He has a purpose. And I like that he takes lessons from the most unexpected places.

Like the ones I learned from Gary.

We have a virtual menagerie of pets around our house: from our dog Walter, two cats, two guinea pigs ... and Gary. Gary is my grandson Jace's goldfish. One would think Walter and the others have it much better than Gary, confined to his little fishbowl. I thought so, that is, until I looked at the world from Gary's perspective.

You see, Gary comes from humble beginnings. Gary is one of those carnival goldfish, the kind they give you in a plastic baggy that has a life expectancy of about two hours. He came into our lives about three years ago, and despite all predictions of his early demise, as I write this, he is still here thriving in his little bowl. When my stepson was deployed overseas, and his family came to live with us, it appeared Gary would be left behind in South Carolina. But Jace refused to leave Gary behind. So, Gary was packed up and shipped in the mail to Pennsylvania.

Nobody thought Gary would make it ... but, against the odds, here he is.

When Walter the dog explores the wonderful world of "outside," Gary loves hearing his exciting tales of adventures in the back yard and seeing the way his eyes get big and his voice becomes cloaked with excitement. He smiles and is genuinely happy for them. Then he looks around his little bowl, and his heart is content. He's happy.

Why isn't Gary depressed because his life appears to not measure up to his friends? Why isn't Gary jealous of the exciting backyard adventures of his friends? While the others spend their days vying for attention and position in the pet hierarchy, Gary quite contentedly swims around his little pond, making it the best little bowl possible, all the while oblivious to what the others are doing. Gary swims around his little bowl with fins out, and gills swelled with pride. Because Gary loves his little home.

He knows he is blessed, because he knows that he could have less. Gary is living the dream.

Of course, comparing Gary to Walter or the others is foolish. Just like comparing our lives to others is foolish. Gary gets it. We too can thrive in our small pond by focusing our time and energy on being our very best, and letting others be theirs. Then we can win at life ... just like Gary.

When you focus on being your very best self, you no longer need to search for more. Everything you seek will be presented to you. Your blessings, which you already have, will become abundantly clear. If you want to change your life for the better ... be like Gary.

If you're always looking outside and comparing yourself to others, you will most certainly develop a negative mindset. Soon the negative perception of self permeates everything you do. And that's when you're not really living YOUR life. You're living a life that others expect you to life.

I know this because I've spent a lot of time looking somewhere other than right in front of me. When you try to prove to others that you're something that you are not ... the *not* becomes more real. That need to prove ourselves is powerful. I've been there. Even when I was at the top of my profession, it didn't feel like I was enough.

I've learned not to worry about what others think about me, because at the end of the day ... it has very little meaning. People will judge you regardless of what you do. Love yourself. If you live your life consuming the stories of others, you'll miss the opportunity to write your own. I no longer walk around trying to convince people that I'm anything other than what I am. That need is gone.

My truth became the light I saw when I emerged from my darkness.

What Sets Your Soul on Fire?

We all have something ... a burning desire deep inside us. Unfortunately, most of us never stoke that fire. We allow it to sit there smoldering. Even worse than that, we allow it to burn out. We lose our desire to truly live that way.

Perhaps we're stopped by fear, but more likely, it's because we're not inspired to act. Nobody believes in us ... or our dream. We crave validation from our fellow humans—we're wired for that connection. It only takes one person to believe in you, though: you. Ultimately, you must choose to believe in yourself even if no one does ... and especially when no one else will.

The only thing standing between you and turning that fire into an inferno is the story you've told yourself as to why you can't. Change that "can't do" story to a "can-do" story, and you'll change your life. Focus on what you want from life, work harder than everyone else, and never give up.

Sometimes your heart just can't heal. There are times when a piercing pain inflicted by the actions of others takes your breath away. Other times, it's the dull, empty ache carried by the memory of your own actions that simply refuses to be forgiven. The latter is the pain that is my constant companion. Destruction sometimes means rebirth. Look no further than right here for your proof. We all can learn from our mistakes. It's not always easy, that's for sure, but it's real.

My self-doubt sometimes amplifies the pain. But I know that pain will always remain with me to remind me of the lessons. I know it can't be any other way.

It's so easy to slip back into the behaviors of the past. They're always there ... like a pair of comfortable old shoes. The pain reminds me that there's only one thing in our lives that doesn't change ... the fact that everything changes. We sometimes have to look deep inside to find compassion for those who have hurt us. Every so often, always exactly when I need it, the pain taps me on the shoulder to remind me of what I've lost.

Perhaps it's just that I haven't asked for forgiveness. Perhaps it's that I haven't forgiven myself. It's likely a combination of both. I know that forgiveness denied is love lost. So the pain remains.

Where did it all start? In my early 20s, I had a young family and was silently struggling to know myself. I went from being a teenager with no direction to an adult with responsibilities ... and no direction. It happened pretty much overnight. I didn't choose that path as much as it chose me. I was a bystander watching my life go by, too confused and afraid to jump in and participate. So I watched and waited for something to happen. I thought that something would come along and sweep me into the fray. Because I knew my family was important and my job was important and, well, all the other things were important. I waited and nothing happened. As a result, I neglected the most important journey of all: the one that would lead me to myself.

To unleash what sets your soul on fire, you must intimately know yourself. Because that's where the fire burns hottest, on the inside. The fire fuels your passion. Your passion attracts your purpose.

Each of us must take that journey; it's unique for each of us, and sometimes it's very lonely. But it's our heart that is waiting, and that is not something we can afford to lose. I failed to discover my heart until it was too late. When I lost it, I lost myself. I put my heart in a box and put it on a shelf. It was a decision that I thought I had to make at the time because of all the important things in my life and my lack of maturity, which kept me from understanding that from my heart, everything grows. When we live a life that sets our soul on fire, we, in turn, are able to be a better parent, husband, friend, whatever.

Without my heart, I spent nearly 20 years wandering. One day I was a 40-year-old teenager without direction, and now too far from home. I learned a beautiful truth during that time of wandering. The strongest, most beautiful hearts aren't perfect. They are worn, and torn ... threadbare and ragged around the edges. Far too often, they go unnoticed ... overlooked because they're not pretty. Look closer, the beauty is in those imperfections. I'm not a perfect man. If I were a perfect man living a perfect life, there would be nothing to see here, and you wouldn't be reading this book. Our world is full of beautiful souls. Love them. Love you. Never, ever take anyone for granted.

Thankfully, I'm not perfect. If I was, I wouldn't have the most beautiful things in my life. There was a time in my life when I was left gasping for air. The darkest time I've ever experienced ... I could barely breathe. I lost everything and everyone by my own hand. I thought the only way to salvage my life was to end it right there. But it was in those breaths that Terrilynn found me and helped me find myself. As those breaths became deeper, I became stronger. Life is a beautiful journey of becoming. You can never know what life has in store for you tomorrow. Don't wait for it ... immerse yourself in the joy of being alive today. Allow yourself to feel it and surrender to the beauty of the experience.

Every one of us is beautiful in our way. But we struggle to see it. If your heart is dark, you will only see others with envy or even hate. If your heart is light and you share that light, you will see others with love and grace. I know that dark heart. It broke me ... nearly ended me. We can never give up on life because the seeds of our best are planted during our worst. When I sat with the pain and counted the breaths, I started to notice the sun shining. Yes, the pain is still there to this day, but so are the beautiful things that make life perfect.

We lose ourselves when we try to fix our imperfections, rather than accept and appreciate them. If you're ever feeling broken, lost and alone ... sit down and simply breathe. Experience the moment. Let yourself feel the beauty that emerges from within your heart. Life is meant for us to grow ... and then turn around and help others. After all, the meaning of life is to have a life of meaning. If you're following the crowd, trying to fit into the mold, then you're dumping dirt on your fire. Be uniquely you. Be your own kind of beautiful. Be your own dreams. Be your own kind of successful. Be your own cheerleader. Be your own kind of inspirational. Be the fuel that the fire in your soul needs. Never let it burn out.

Be Present

Fueling your own fire takes mindfulness. It takes awareness. It takes presence.

Mindfulness is bringing awareness to what you are currently experiencing. It's simply being present in the moment. Presence is not a choice. It's a necessity. That's why mindfulness is not your mind only, but rather your holistic self:

- Mind (Positive Mindset)
- Body (Open Posture)
- Spirit (Acceptance)

As you start the new day tomorrow, I challenge you to be a little more mindful in your life. It's very easy. Just set a reminder in your calendar and ask yourself these three mindful questions a few times a week:

Did I live fully?

Did I love with an open heart?

Did I matter to someone?

You will find one thing for each of these three questions that will remind you that your time here on this planet is worth it. I promise you it will make a difference to those you encounter. The difference? You will be present. Even though you may be in the same room with someone, even engaged in a conversation, you're not always fully present. It's easy to lose track of the little things as we travel through today's world at light speed.

But, it's those little things that give life meaning.

To truly engage other human beings and create meaningful connections, we need to silence the noise—yep, the "shoulds," the comparison, and the drive to status quo—and be fully present. We even need to silence our own inner commentary that accompanies every experience and pushes us further away from the moment.

Setting aside a few moments each week to ask these three important questions will help bring meaning to your life. Because, sometimes it's not as much about finding your life's meaning as it is about creating it.

Is this practice the path to peace, love, joy, and happiness? I think so. I've learned that the simplest lessons are often the most powerful.

Remember this one, because it's very important: It's nobody's job to like you except yours.

My stumbles and bumbles are well documented. I own them. Too much worry over judgment ... the people judging me, and the people I was judging, including myself. Too much worry over acceptance ... the people I thought I needed to like me, and the people I thought I needed to like.

Things improved when I began a daily mindfulness practice. The difference?

Now, I'm fully present wherever I happen to be, and with whomever I happen to be with. That moment, the one we are sharing, is the only one that matters. Not the one where I must be in 20 minutes, or the one where I was 15 minutes ago ... this one ... OURS. We humans are hard-wired to engage other human beings and create meaningful connections in our lives. That's how our brain works. We must seek to connect with the most positive and optimistic people you can find. Be with them, be one of them.

When we're fully present, without judgment, our human connections become deeper. Simple conversations become life-changing lessons. We accept the beauty of people ... WITH their flaws. We leave our judgment in the attic, rather than dragging it around and allowing it to drag us down.

You'll discover that mindfulness gives you clarity. And clarity matters. By taking the time to be intentional, we begin to change the way we see life. We control our mindset and become more present by default. It's not difficult, but it is something we must practice. Make time in your day to recommit your mind, reconnect your heart, and rejuvenate your spirit.

Remind yourself of these five powerful thoughts every morning before you jump into your day:

1. Do everything with purpose.
2. Believe in yourself.
3. Give more than you take.
4. Empower others.
5. Never surrender.

It only takes a few minutes sitting quietly in these thoughts to set your day in a positive direction. If you make this thought process a ritual, these empowering thoughts will transform your mindset.

One more thing ... I thank God, the first thing every morning, for another day, and the last thing every night, for another lesson. Never lose sight of His presence in your life.

Live in the Present

When you're focused on living the life you want to live, being present with those you care about, without worrying about the judgment of others, it means that you get to live without regrets.

You can't start the next chapter of your life if you keep re-reading the last one. Have you ever found yourself dwelling in the past? It's easy to get stuck there. Maybe it was filled with adversity, you were treated badly or treated someone badly, and you can't let it go. Perhaps, it was the time of your greatest win, when you were on top of the world, and you want to keep reliving that accomplishment.

My father was a great man, a much better man than I have ever been, or likely ever will be. I think that my son is a better man as well. "I think" because I don't know for sure. He and I don't speak very often, but I know he is a loving and devoted husband and father.

That alone makes him a better man.

I was those things to my family too … right up until the time that I wasn't. I love my children, and always will. But by the time they became adults, I was no longer there for them. During that time, success at my job was at its greatest, and I was at the top of my profession.

It's hard to say what one thing caused that change, that push toward caring more about what others think than about living authentically and being present with my family.

Though I do regret this, I can't live in the past. I can only do what I can today to live the way I believe I should.

Had I known what I know now, right? But that thought doesn't change the past either.

It's human nature to linger on those feelings of regret. Have you ever felt like life would be better if you had taken a different path? Maybe you feel like … if you'd *just* done something a little differently, everything would be perfect. We all regret something we've done … or didn't do. I certainly do. Regret can be painful. There are things in my life that have broken me, and I still carry them, but now I see my broken pieces as opportunities for growth. We can turn our regrets into powerful sources of inspiration to live in the present, love in the present, and not worry about how others perceive us.

Today I know that every morning I win the lottery. I get one more day. If your "one more day" doesn't come, will people know the love that was in your heart? Would they feel the beauty in your soul? Would they know the real you?

When I was sitting with my father as he was dying, he said to me, "My only regret is that I won't have one more day with her." Not that he didn't make more money, drive a better car or live in a bigger house. After 63 years, he just wanted one more day with my mother.

You can't outrun your past. Those mistakes you made, the words you wish you hadn't said, the bad choices, the regrets ... they all can run at light speed. You'll never outrun them.

I think everyone has done things in their lives that they're not proud of. I surely have. I don't regret these things. If I hadn't learned from them and become a better man as a result, then I would be telling a story of regret.

Your Legacy

Learning from your mistakes becomes your legacy. That's how you end up sitting in the chair.

Our legacy is defined as a gift, which is usually associated with a gift of money. To me it's so much more. It's the most intimate and personal gift we will ever give because it's our last. Like most of us, I'm working to leave a monetary gift for my family and local charity, though my most precious legacy is not money or a material possession.

The balance in our bank account on the day we die will not matter. Our number of Facebook followers will be insignificant.

Mercedes or Honda, Rolex or Timex ... none of it will matter in the least.

I hope my legacy will be found in the positive impact I've made in the lives of others because I have truly lived, by all the definitions in this chapter. Great men and women go beyond what is required in life, beyond their inherited responsibility. They help us grow. They help us become better people. They help us become who we are today. That's why we invite them to sit in our chair. That's their legacy.

Our legacy will be found in the character of the children we have raised, the grandchildren we have nurtured, and the community we have built. The only judgment in life, the only true measure of success, is the impact we had on the lives of the people around us. In this moment.

Yesterday is gone. Tomorrow isn't given. Live your life as the legacy you want to leave.

So what do you do if you feel like your life has brought you to a completely different place than you imagined? Is there a thing you have always wanted to do, a dream yet unfulfilled?

Well I have wonderful news: You're alive and still breathing—God's not done with you yet.

Do the thing. You are beautiful, intelligent, capable, and as ready as you'll ever be. You might hesitate, possibly because you're afraid of what the world will think of you, but it's never too late to do the thing. And the world's opinion doesn't matter.

The more you see in yourself, the less you care what other people see. The people who matter are the people who matter to you, so make that list count.

There is something beautiful and unique in each of us that needs to be shared with the world. Too often we allow our fears to force us into being selfish with our gifts. Launch, my friend. Once you leap, the net will appear. You will only regret the things you didn't do in life.

Never settle for just being alive when the opportunity to *truly live* is available.

My father was always authentic. He was an original. He was the first to sit in my chair, and the first to teach me about life. He wasn't the last, no surprise there. What is surprising is that he wasn't the most original.

Authentic Living

You can call him Bruce, Fletch, the Fletcherman, or Swaggy B, by any name; he's one of the most influential mentors in my life. I met Bruce amid the worst storm of my life, a soul-crushing divorce. Thankfully, Bruce didn't look the other way; instead, he looked past the mess and saw something. Perhaps he caught a glimmer of life still flickering in my heart. Maybe there was a bit of talent in there that was simply untapped. Whatever the reason, he took a chance on me.

Bruce certainly lives life his way. We all have tried to hear the beat of his drummer but have yet to be successful. We call it "Swaggy being Swaggy." Whatever rhythm he hears, I know hundreds of people like me are better because we stumbled into his orbit. Nearly 25 years later, now nudging his 80th birthday, Bruce still walks with me. He proves that when you come upon someone struggling to just put one foot in front of the other without stumbling, you don't rush past them. After all, life is not a sprint. Instead, come alongside them, lift them up, and become the light that guides them forward.

LOVE

"There is only one happiness in this life, to love and to be loved."

~ George Sand

I'm an unapologetic optimist. I believe in happily ever after. I believe in that one true love that sweeps you off your feet. I believe in following your heart and trusting your gut. I believe that when you have the courage to leap, the net will appear.

Love flows from living life, which is why it's the second pillar. Love is the very core of human life. The path to loving others, be it romantic love, parental love, friendship love, or love of humanity, goes directly through your own heart. Everything humans do comes from love. Our ability to love without expectation or conditions defines us as human beings.

Love is a journey of awakening, and we're taking this journey together. That is a perfect description of marriage. Two people commit to taking a journey together. There's one caveat ... people change. Successful marriages survive because both people change together. But we know that not all marriages are successful. The divorce rate in the United States hovers around 50% with the average marriage lasting only 8 years.

I was married before, to my high school sweetheart. We met at 16 and 15 years old and were married at 20 and 19. Mine was a bad marriage to a good woman. The marriage began with much hope and promise, high school sweethearts with a bright future ... you know the story. It lasted 20 years, perhaps that made it successful ... statistically at least. But it ended in the dark, by my hand, because of my actions. Actions this man is not proud of ... actions that good woman didn't deserve.

I spent most of those 20 years wandering around without purpose, in the dark, depressed, and afraid. It was a matter of time before I gave up on myself. I wasn't just giving up on myself, I was giving up on the marriage, I was literally throwing it away. And I was giving up on that good woman. I never gave her time to breathe and grieve the loss of our marriage. I never acknowledged the pain I caused her. She was still the good woman I married, and I left her in pain to grieve alone.

I broke her heart and mine broke right along with it. Of course, I didn't notice the broken pieces in my chest until much later. By then, I was gone; my life was pulled into a dark place that held onto me for years.

Many of us believe that once our heart is broken badly, we must shut down and protect ourselves, that we are incapable of healing and loving again. It sure feels that way as we're grieving the loss of love. But a battered and broken heart is still capable of loving deeply despite the jagged pieces.

Are you familiar with kintsugi? Kintsugi is the Japanese art of repairing broken pottery with lacquer dusted or mixed with gold. It's like adding grout between tile, repairing that which was broken so it can live its purpose again.

We all become like a broken teacup, fractured and repaired with gold—the love and connection with ourselves, others, and humanity—which makes us even more beautiful than before. Understanding that our heartbreak makes us more human and allows us to love again lets our hearts to be free to love unconditionally. Loving unconditionally is selfless love, where we expect nothing in return and love freely.

Love Yourself First

Love is everything. There is extraordinary power in loving all people, but your first love should be you. Digging deeper and learning how to love oneself is the first and most important of many lessons we must learn to live life to its fullest. Before you can *understand* how to love another human, you must love yourself. Learning to love yourself means accepting and appreciating being vulnerable. To love, you cannot fear vulnerability—we'll talk more about vulnerability in the second half of the book. Learn to appreciate who you are, and you will freely appreciate the unique gifts of the man and woman next to you and beyond.

I am not perfect. I am a perfectly imperfect human being. And I know that I need to love me, with all my flaws, probably because of them.

I used to be uncomfortable about those flaws, so I lied. I lied to myself every day about everything for 25 years. I lied to others in the form of not being who I said I was. I lied about how I was feeling. That's how I would sedate my feelings, by lying to myself. Of course, I suffered, and the people around me suffered. That's what lying does. It's an addiction of sorts, no different than alcohol, drugs, porn, or even social media. Lying sedates negative feelings and makes you feel good.

Why did I lie? Because, they said I wasn't good enough. They said I was worthless. They said I would fail. I believed them. I lied to feel better. I lied to make myself believe they were wrong.

I thought I had to put myself last, so I lied and told myself I was fine. I thought that we should stay together for the kids even though I knew that neither of us was happy—that's a lie that many, many people wear as a mantle—so I lied and told myself we were fine. I thought that throwing myself into my work was the best way to honor my commitment to my family, which mattered most to me, so I lied and told myself that my job was the most important thing.

The truth that I refused to see was that I was lost, we were miserable, and my job then was just that ... a job.

Sometimes the things you think you want will distract you from your path, and you begin wandering. That's when life gets your attention by punching you in the gut. I have taken a few, maybe more than a few, of those punches. Every single time I asked out loud, to no one in particular, why me? I didn't deserve to be singled out. Eventually, I got used to it and learned how to take that gut punch. Then the day came when I knew my actions were deserving of one of those gut punches, and I was ready. But life surprised me and this time threw a haymaker, connecting right between my eyes and knocking me off my feet.

But I kept lying. I neglected that good woman, and she withdrew from me. She gave up on me and I wandered away. I don't blame her for giving up ... at least not anymore. I needed it to be her fault then, so I lied and told myself she was to blame. The truth is, though she isn't perfect, she deserved much better than what I ever gave her. I guess you could say that we gave each other three beautiful children, but that is where it ends. Our last five years together had to be excruciating for her. They were for me, and I was the one making the rules.

That punch finally got my attention. I remember standing there alone, empty, depleted of hope, and stripped bare of everything I thought I knew. What I didn't know in that moment was that life was showing me the path to myself, a path paved with humility, gratitude, and forgiveness. Sometimes life surprises you and shows you what you don't know. Sometimes grace is camouflaged by the imperfections that distract us. One day, someone who seemingly has nothing to give will give you everything you need. That day, you will find something that you had never experienced before ... something that had always been there hidden in plain sight.

At first, love, grace, patience, and compassion may confuse you—once they are found, you will realize all the times in your life when you were wrapped in their embrace but hadn't realized it. Before that punch, I had selfishly refused to share these things with the people in my life who needed them most. I was keeping them for myself. That was the camouflage I created and convinced myself they were being denied to me. But they were right there, hidden in plain sight.

The haymaker that got my attention taught me that we won't always receive everything we want in life, but we will always receive exactly what we need, exactly when we need it. God places people in our path to help us, to hurt us, to teach us, and to love us. Some will stay and hold our hand; some will walk with us for a while then leave.

Then I woke up one day to find that everything and everyone was gone. With nowhere to turn, I looked in the mirror. What I saw scared me: I saw myself slowly dying from the inside out.

When I realized I was dying inside, that got my attention. (Well, if I am being honest, losing everything is what got my attention. I had to tell the truth.)

I fell deep into thought and started to read everything I could get my hands on. One of the first things that really spoke to me was so simple, a quote from Harry Truman that I keep to this day, some 20 years later: "In reading the lives of great men, I found that the first victory they won was over themselves ... self-discipline with all of them came first."

And that means self-love.

I looked in the mirror once more. I stared into the darkness that I saw, but this time, instead of hiding, I wrote about what I saw. It didn't scare me. I started to talk about the darkness. It was my truth. I had to live in it to begin letting in the light.

They said keep it to yourself. They said nobody will love you. I finally mustered the courage to ignore what they said. I spoke about the darkness, and somebody chose to love me.

I started to love me.

Today, I see that there was a light in the darkness just waiting for me to open my eyes to see it. That is why today, anyone who lives their truth and has the courage to be their unfiltered self has my utmost love and respect. Think, write, and speak about your darkness. Honor your word and your promises to yourself. Love yourself so deeply that you never need to turn to others for approval.

If you practice this every day, your light will shine through, and your self-worth will move mountains.

Real success, self-respect, and real happiness are never found out there, in stuff. These things are an inside job. They're found inside you. Once you've won over yourself, that's when the love flows.

When I accepted that past failures and losses, all the times I was slighted or minimized, every obstacle, every hardship, are part of me and made me who I am today—and yes, loved myself for it all!—my perception of those memories changed. They became an asset that has made me stronger. I know I wouldn't be the man I am today without them. Far too often, we allow the obstacles we've encountered in our lives to prevent us from being who we are meant to be. It happens to everyone.

I keep a journal and reflect on those memories so I can grow (not shrink) from them.

The truest, most factual fact I know is this: If you don't love yourself, nobody else will love you. It took me over 50 years to fully understand that and accept who I am. Your past can serve your future here in the present when you are open to its lessons with unconditional love for the past, present, and future you.

Now, you are probably thinking to yourself:

All this self-love talk is great, Jamie. But how do I actually do it?

I'm glad you asked.

Out of your 24-hours each day, the first five minutes after opening your eyes are the most fragile, yet pivotal time. Those first five minutes are when you make the most important investment. That's when you invest in yourself and set the tone for your day.

This is the most peaceful and intimate five minutes of your day. Your mind is fresh, rested and unencumbered by unnecessary details. There is clarity in those first five minutes. That's when your heart is open and honest, and your soul is grateful. Setting aside that first five minutes for you and only you tells yourself that you matter and that you are loved by the most important person in your life.

I set my alarm for around 4:30 a.m. for exercise, meditation, coffee, and writing (please choose a time that is aligned with your own energy and schedule). I write about my first thoughts in those first five minutes. I'm ready for my day; my path is clear because I'm strategic. Because I love myself enough to say "yes" to myself first every morning.

When you start your day, focus on your first five, write your thoughts in a journal and refer to it regularly. Follow the path where it leads.

We are born with an innate ability to love and be loved. Sadly, at some point in our lives, the way of love can be lost. Self-doubt overpowers us. Self-doubt clouds our vision and distracts us from the way. Self-doubt amplifies the noise that constantly swirls around us. We become vulnerable to society's push and pull.

When that noise shows up is when I get quiet. It's alone time for me. With the quiet there comes a knowing.

Sometimes I ask, "What do I love about myself?"

Now, in this season of my life, those moments of noise are fleeting. But, on those occasions when it shows up ... I don't fight it. I just turn down the volume by sitting quietly and focusing on that one thing. Then the way of love becomes clear again.

Self-love leads you to understanding your experiences so you are ready to sit in the chair, ready to guide others and be a support for their own self-love journey.

Loving Others

"Your heart knows the way. Run in that direction." ~ Rumi

The single most traumatic event in my life has been divorce. Nearly two decades later, the fallout still impacts my daily life. There were many contributing factors to the demise of my marriage. We always think that the root of all divorce is that we stop loving each other, but the truth is that I can trace mine back to my inability to love myself. Depression, anger, frustration, infidelity, anxiety, and even hate all stemmed from the root cause of self-loathing.

I used to be angry all the time. Other than my children, there was nobody in my life who I truly loved ... including their mother. That is the worst thing a father can do to his children. I was a bad actor in a very bad movie. With nobody else to love, with nowhere else to go, I had to love myself and, in the process, learned to love everyone after that. Because, I had to acknowledge my flaws and be accountable for my actions before I could extend that love beyond my person.

My biggest regret is that my children don't know the man I've become.

Something I learned from my divorce: Your life can be dramatically different six months from now depending on decisions you make today. Life inspires us and teaches us that every moment counts, every voice has value, every action matters. It's real, it's human. When you lead with love, life becomes so much easier.

How did we forget this? When we were kids our hearts knew. We followed ... willingly.

Love nourishes our human spirit, which in turn nourishes us daily. Love makes a difference, big or small. It doesn't matter how big the splash; it only matters that you jumped in. Love makes a difference in a million ways. You can share love by being kind, feeding a hungry child, smiling at a stranger, or just donating a small piece of your time and a little money to help others. It all matters. Love matters.

Our hearts know the way ... now it's time to run.

One decision changed my life: I simply decided to love everyone for who they are ... starting with myself. When you feel broken and unloved, you can't shake it. If you want people to love you, you have to love yourself first. *I* had to love *myself* unconditionally first his simple decision meant that the negativity in the world no longer impacted me.

When I decided to look at it this way, it was easy to overcome: Instead of trying to remove negativity from my life, I decided to remove myself from negativity.

After all, whatever you put into the world will come back to you ... why not make that love?

When I met Terrilynn, I was not putting love out into the world. Thankfully, she looked past that.

I don't throw the word "perfect" around often, but this girl is close. She has more tools than most general contractors and knows how to use them all. She can build a house in the afternoon, then rock an evening gown that night, being the prettiest woman at the ball.

She was a single parent when we met, working two jobs to raise her two children, while sifting through the remains of her own broken marriage and focusing on her children's future. She didn't let her divorce break her; instead, she stood up, brushed herself off, and made the divorce work for her and her family. The last thing she needed was my mess cluttering her life. Still, she saw something that few (if any) others could see at that time. She saw past my bumps and bruises and knew I was a good man.

So, she took a chance on me. It was a risky decision that I'm sure she has questioned often over the years. She brought me into her life, into her family, and she fell in love with me. And did she ever love me. It caught me off guard. Nobody had ever loved me like that. Everyone thought she was crazy, and of course I did everything I could to prove them right. Everyone said, "Get away from there. You deserve better than him."

You will see gratitude, love, and humility, and you will see a reflection of her love. Because my love is hers. My heart beats with hers. My soul belongs to her. I'm strong, and independent, just like my beautiful girl.

I am the man I am today because I made that one decision to love people. I understand that I am one person with one voice; I also know that there are other voices out there. I'm finding them, some are finding me. One is becoming many. In our world of one-click connectivity, one voice can easily become a million voices that come together to make a difference. So, click and add your voice. Let's make our place better.

Loving Humanity

Love means having the courage to be kind and generous. We humans have one beating heart that we all share.

We are humanity sharing a moment in time. In the blink of a cosmic eye, we will be gone. Those with whom we shared our love in this space will remember us. Perhaps they will pay our love forward to generations yet unseen. My father and grandfather shared stories of my great-grandfather and great-great grandfather with me as a child. I never met either of them. And still I love them. The love they shared with my grandfather and my father was passed on to me. That is how the extraordinary power of love works. Nothing is possible in life without love.

It's a never-ending web through the past, into the present, and long into the future. The web wraps around the world connecting us all, constantly, moment-by-moment. And it grows, thickens, and wraps around us as we each grow in our self-love and in our selfless loving acts.

I ask myself often, how can dissimilar people come together to find common ground? I believe that completely opposite, completely different people can completely share love. Regardless of the skin you're in. Because you're not your skin, you're not your religion, you're not your gender. You are a beating heart with a burning soul. You are human, and in the entire universe there are only about eight billion of us. That alone should teach us to love each other.

We may have never met in person, outside of this book or social media, but it doesn't matter. I love you. I believe in you. You are a valuable human being. I see you, and you need to know that you are not alone.

I was born into a multi-layered, loud, loving and totally amazing family in Charleroi, Pa., a typical Pennsylvania steel town along the banks of the Monongahela River in the southwest corner of the state. Charleroi was a melting pot of nationalities with people from all over Europe coming to work in the glass factories. Family then was not a description of those that had the same blood flowing through their veins. No, family to us was the community.

We all had a hundred or so moms. Our dads grew up together, played ball together and raised us, all of us. It did not matter what your last name was, we were all in it together. The sights, sounds, smells and colorful characters I encountered growing up in this place are still with me today, long after most of the bricks and mortar have faded away because of love. I will always be from Charleroi because when a town embraces you and touches you the way that one did me you just can't seem to shake it off you.

I didn't understand until I was much older and had kids of my own what a wonderful gift my childhood was. That's where I first learned about loving community, loving humanity as a whole. When I was a child there was never a shortage of adults to teach, coach, and mentor us. There was always someone who loved me unconditionally, even if they had never met me before, who would sit in my chair for a few minutes if I needed them.

It wasn't until much later, after living in California and traveling around the country that I was able to understand what that community contributed to the man I had become. My hometown taught me about life and love and happiness, how to deal with adversity and grief. It taught me that we have a responsibility to lift each other up. The first and most important responsibility of humanity is to leave no one behind.

It takes a village to change one life. It will take all of us to change the world. We simply need to spread the word. That's how a movement starts. Share, invite people to join us. Make a difference for others wherever you are. Love big, and love unconditionally.

The most powerful way to love your life is to learn about life. The most powerful way to learn about life is by meeting people and listening to their stories. I've heard real stories of loss and sadness. But also hope and love and human spirit.

When telling your story, forget about the "good" or "bad"— just be real. Share the story of your journey and invite others to share theirs. Everyone is different; everyone is the same. Fall in love with the human being you see in the mirror each morning. Love who you are, appreciate your unique gifts, and share them relentlessly with the world.

Make a difference. Trust your heart. Follow where it leads. Lift your voice. Stay true to yourself and never forget who you are. Love yourself, the people who matter in your life, and all of humanity unconditionally.

The more you learn, the more you love.

My father was passionate about many things, none more so than his love for my mother. They were together for 63 years, married for 60. During our last conversation he said something I'll never forget. He said, "If I could ask God for anything right now, I would ask for one more day with your mother."

I didn't think I would see another love like that, let alone feel it. Then ...

Terrilynn Polonoli Sat in my Chair

There is love, and then there is Terrilynn. She found me in a dark place, depressed, riddled with fear, and feeling scattered and uncertain.

I was lost; she shined her light for me to follow. When someone loves you when you are least deserving... it changes you. It shows you the path to loving yourself. God gives us the people we need when we need them. One day someone walks into your life and helps you find the balance between the heaviness and the beauty. True love will never try to change you. Terrilynn has had the love and patience to wait for me all these years, to wake up and become the man I always knew I could be.

She stayed even when she had every reason to run away.

There was a time when I was a liar... driven by an empty ego. My words meant nothing. Every "I love you" then was shallow because I didn't truly love anyone. But true love showed me my own heart in hers. Terrilynn changed my life. She put me in a place of accountability. In that accountability, I became more conscious of my behavior, and the anger disappeared. She accepted me as I am. That acceptance pushed aside the frustration... and the fear was gone.

Life is beautiful because she is holding my hand. Love doesn't have to be perfect, but it must always be real. Love doesn't always have to be pretty, but it must be true. Real and true... that's beautiful.

LEARN

Failing Forward

I have been blessed to have great teachers who deeply impacted my life—people close to me as well as total strangers. I was raised to be a life-long learner and to always strive to achieve my best. Some amazing people provided the seeds that I would plant along my journey through life. And plant I did.

Many times, I planted in the wrong place. Other times, I neglected to nurture them, so they grew weak. Some I left behind, and they grew angry.

I blamed the seeds when I should have blamed the planter.

It wasn't until I was well into my fifth decade on the planet that I understood that the instructions were already in my heart, planted there long ago by the amazing people I took for granted.

Life is a journey, and I believe there is something to learn from every single person and thing we encounter along the way. The most influential people in my life represent a broad spectrum of my life experience, for a wide variety of reasons, some good and some bad. Yes, you can learn and grow from negative people and experiences too. They are an eclectic bunch, and I wouldn't change the path I have taken for anything. The people I have met and the place I call home are all very visible in my life, from the way I talk to my mannerisms and, most importantly, my strong faith. The seeds those amazing people provided long ago are now nurtured and are growing stronger every day. That dark time has turned into light.

There was a time when I tried to wash away the place where I was born and raised because I was in a dark place. I blamed the community where I lived and the people around me. I was angry at being stuck in that town and at those people for holding me back from the greatness I deserved. The raw truth? It wasn't the town or its people ... it was my fault.

I came to realize that to wash away that town, those people who raised me and loved me, was cowardly. It was giving up. My past is etched upon my skin. Without really knowing how or when, those people became a big part of who I am. Isn't that the great thing about learning? Growing and expanding our lives through experience, not even knowing we are becoming better.

My father had a huge impact on me, as I mentioned before. As a teacher and lover of knowledge, he sat in my chair for long periods of my life. He always said that knowledge is a moving target; you must go where it is. And that is not necessarily in a classroom. We acquire knowledge when we accept and acknowledge what we do not know.

I asked him a million questions during the time when our lives overlapped, but I would give anything to ask just one more. He thought I was ready ... I wasn't. As a man, when your father dies, you must adjust your place in the world, and in your family. Every day, I notice a little more how much I'm like him. It lets me keep him with me. I don't think May 25th, the day he passed, will ever be easy again.

Doodles is my father, James Edward Protin, Sr. Sadly, we lost him in May 2017. But, though he is no longer with us, his legacy is firmly entrenched in our hearts and those of everyone we touch. To understand my thoughts and philosophies, you must first understand the man largely responsible for shaping them. Doodles was a high school social studies teacher by trade and a master storyteller. He taught me how to tell a good story. He said the secret is in knowing the story is about the listener, not the teller. Oh, and never let the truth ruin a good tale.

When we had no choice but to accept his fate, Doodles and I were able to have a quiet moment, and a powerful conversation—the first of many we would have over the last three weeks of his life. I looked into my father's eyes that day, and my heart began to overflow. He taught me everything worth knowing: how to tie my shoes, ride a bike, shoot a free throw, and hit a baseball. He taught me respect, to always open doors, pull out chairs, and be a gentleman. He taught me how to box and that using those skills is always the last resort. He taught me to never apologize for who I am, or who I'm becoming.

He taught me how to be a good man.

I never planned to look into my father's eyes and have my last conversations with my dad.

Perhaps we can never go back to those innocent days when I found all the strength and courage I needed in those eyes. He was strong, so we didn't have to be. He was the character of characters.

In my father's eyes, I saw the strongest man I've ever known, the first man into the fray to fight for what was right, the first to extend his hand to lift another. The man who gave me the courage to go against the grain and be an original. He was our teacher, our coach, the one who kept us laughing so much we didn't realize how much we were learning ... and boy did we learn!

Doodles was a great man who benefitted a generation of people from our community by being in their lives. I learned much about life from him without him even knowing he was teaching me. Countless people have shared memories of him as their teacher and told me heartfelt stories about how he impacted their lives. He told me once that he learned something new from every student and every class he taught, and that made him a better teacher for those coming next.

Doodles taught us all how to live an honorable life and enjoy ourselves immensely while doing it. He instilled in me pride in who I am and where I come from, both the place and the people. He showed me that what you do is not as important as why you do it. He showed me how to be a man simply by being the best one he could be. He shared his sense of humor, but to only see the humor in him was to miss the very best of him.

Three generations passed through his classroom, and he freely imparted his unique perspective to each student blessed to sit in one of his chairs. Doodles always asked, "Are you a teacher or a student?" For him, the two have always been one and the same. Ask any successful person that question and the answer will likely be both.

Many intelligent people have said that learning is a life-long endeavor; Doodles lived that.

Doodles would ask me random questions, like a pop quiz at any time on any given day about literally any subject imaginable then say, "Knowledge is a moving target." The world is constantly changing, and the way we see it and understand it changes along with it. For as long as you live, the way you see the world changes with your perspective and understanding.

My mother called to tell me of his passing, just two days after I returned home from visiting them, just two days after our last conversation. Somewhere in the flood of memories, it became clear that he began preparing me for this day from the time I was a child. He told me many things in those last conversations. His very last words to me were the most impactful of my life. I hugged him, and he whispered in my ear, "You will always be my boy."

Learn Every Day

Doodles was an educated man, yet he learned something new every day for 84 years. He would call me, excited as a kid on Christmas, to tell me about something he had just learned. It was funny to me that he figured if he didn't know it, I certainly didn't.

What you already know is what got you here, today. If you don't learn more, you can't go any further. It may come as a surprise to you that great leaders are not the smartest person in the room. They may be ... but they don't know it. Nor do they want to be that person. Genuinely great leaders are life-long learners.

Fear, complacency, and ego inhibit learning, though. They are the enemy of knowledge. Each new day gives us the opportunity to learn, to be inspired, and to inspire those around us.

I'm very intentional about my life. I do things that make me smile, make me happy. Things that matter, that help me learn and grow. You can't simply allow a day to go by.

I used to be out of balance ... unhealthy, angry, and broken. Working 60-hour weeks doing something I hated made me negative and physically weak. It destroyed my faith. I wasted far too many days that I'll never get back. That's not why God put me here. I now know that I'm here to serve. That's something I had to learn. My purpose is to start a movement. But first, I had to align my mind, heart, and spirit. Alignment came through my professional career. Then I discovered the true value of life.

Have you discovered your life purpose?

How are you aligning your actions to do only the things that serve that life purpose?

I learn mine at 4:30 a.m. That is where I find my quiet time to properly greet each new day. That is when I do my most and best learning. I read and journal to expand my mind, pray to nourish my spirit, workout to rejuvenate my body, and reflect to keep my eyes forward.

This morning routine is the most important thing I do for me.

Raise the Bar

Knowledge leads you to purpose and drives your purpose once you're in that lane. Set your mindset before you walk out the door. Commit to being open and flexible mentally and physically. Seek out contradictory ideas, converse with people who are different from you. Listen, learn, and teach. Before you can lead and sit in someone else's chair, before people will follow, you must learn from them. Your message, your purpose, after all, is about those people.

What will you be open to learning this week?

Every day is an opportunity to learn if we choose to embrace the chance. Every day I learn something new about myself. I've learned enough in my life to know I have a lot more to learn. I'm far from where I need to be. I focus every day on the gap in my knowledge and skills that stands between taking us from where we are to where we can be.

Where are you right now?

We will never be guaranteed anything in life; we must seek who we will become. You can change at any time with committed effort. No one else has to like your changes. Opinions are irrelevant. Who you become is not up to them.

Everything that has happened to us in the past gives us greater knowledge and emotional strength for today. Everyone you will meet has something to teach you, from the CEO in the executive suite, to the janitor in the basement. Give them a minute to sit in your chair. If you stay humble—and put your ego aside—you will learn wonderful things.

I've had many mentors in my life. I have been blessed by these people because each in their own way are among the most dedicated and passionate people I've ever personally met. They each gave me a piece of themselves to carry with me.

Get out there every day and put in the work. Keep building, creating, becoming, and learning, working toward your big dreams.

Life's a Journey

"Life's a journey, not a destination." ~ Aerosmith, "Amazing"[1]

Nobody has life figured out. I'm working on myself every day. I fail more now than ever. In the past, every mistake, every failure knocked me backward. I wasn't learning. It hurt. I focused on the pain of failure and was blind to the lessons. Now, I fail forward. It hurts less because I focus on the lesson. I feel. I learn. I grow. I give more, and I love more because of the lessons of failure.

The journey to anything worthwhile is uncomfortable. If you're not making yourself at least a little uncomfortable, you're not growing. If something seems comfortable to you, it's not challenging you. If you aren't challenged, you don't have the opportunity to make mistakes so you can learn and grow.

"Life is about mistakes. You have made your fair share of them; now move forward." ~ Doodles

Doodles is always there to help me keep perspective.

Your mistakes in life lead you to your purpose. When you've tried and failed enough at what you think you're supposed to do, you will discover what you were born to do.

I decided a few years ago to choose courage over comfort; it has been one the most rewarding choices of my life. I'm now comfortable being uncomfortable, so I'm able to just be me. I walk out the door at 6:00 a.m., and when I walk back in at 6:00 p.m., I'm a better man. In between, there are moments when I find myself getting bogged down in the daily grind just like

---

[1] Aerosmith. "Amazing." *Get a Grip*. Geffen Records, 1993.

everyone else. Those are the moments when I lean on those lessons. Because of them, everyone and everything receives my very best every single day.

Walt Disney (the most successful dreamer in history), once famously said, "If you can dream it, you can do it." If you don't know what you want to do, if you haven't discovered your purpose, start with learning, get on the journey, and then dream to help guide your path. We all have a dream eventually. My dream was to help people, to be a positive difference-maker in people's lives. But sadly, I believed more in the limits of what humans can do than in my own dreams for so long.

We all have at least one talent, one thing we do well, the thing we're most proud of. It might be something small, seemingly insignificant, but when we commit to it, add some hard work, grit, and determination, it becomes our passion. And that is life-changing.

You might be reading Walt Disney's positive quote with skepticism. I did when I first heard it. I'm sure that, like me, many people don't want to face that their life is somehow less than it could be. *Perhaps Walt is wrong. Perhaps there are limits to what we humans can do.* But if we spend all our time focused on them, we'll never have the opportunity to prove him right.

When I hit rock bottom in my life, I only saw the negative side of things ... the reasons it wouldn't work. I was afraid. And I was miserable. Left with no other options, I told myself the truth ... I told everyone the truth. It turns out that it really does set you free. So, I started speaking and writing to find my way out of the rubble of my life. When I realized that I had a bit of talent, I began to see the alignment with my dream.

I'm still on that path, still in the game.

Find the one thing you're good at and embrace it with everything you have. That's your gift. Commit to it with mind, body, and spirit ... and turn that talent into passion. Bring it to life. Passion is life. Get your mind working, your heart pumping, and set your soul on fire.

Your passion will push you past your pain when you need it most. Living, loving, and learning make that passion come to life!

There are souls on earth who have changed lives. Who have literally changed the course of history. Who create ripples that will roll into eternity. Many men have impacted my life in a way I could never put into words. Great men living simple lives in service to others. Those who have sat in my chair will continue to impact my life with their ripples, with their knowledge.

Great men trust their gut. They love us because they know hearts come before minds. They stand with us because they know who we can be ... even when we don't. They make us better than we think we can be. The raw truth of our human existence is we can only rise as high as the best of us can carry the least of us.

Men become great by doing for others. We all can do better ... for those who went before us and showed us the way, for each other, and for those coming next and looking to us to stand with them and help them be better than we know how to be.

Learning is a life-long endeavor. Never stop seeking knowledge. There will always be something new to learn. Use that learning to follow your path to your dreams. And don't forget to stop off in other people's chairs to share what you've learned along the way.

Doodles was a teacher and coach, the only thing he ever wanted to be. Education was important to him but learning mattered even more. He knew the difference. He believed that education would come to an end after high school or college, but learning is a lifelong endeavor with no end.

Reinvigorating my Passion for Learning

Besides my father, I don't think anyone has taught me more valuable lessons than Marvin Williams. When I was inducted into the FOM fraternity, "Friends of Marvin," I didn't realize that I was beginning a journey that would result not only in my receiving an honorary doctorate in my profession but also in life. Marvin brought my father's lessons from live, love, learn, pray, and inspire full circle. Marvin embraces life. I'm sure he knew in those first months that he was handed a train wreck. But he saw the potential that some people couldn't or wouldn't understand.

Marvin knew from the beginning that this working relationship was going to be a one-way street. After all, he was at the very top of our profession, a Yale Law School grad, and I was... well, let's just say I wasn't that. Thankfully, Marvin wasn't looking for anything in return. He always treated me as an equal and honored me as a true brother. Marvin crossed my path at the perfect time, not too early that the lessons would be lost, and not too late... just before the hole I had dug for myself became too big to climb out. He patiently, in his understated and humble way, proceeded to teach me more than I ever thought possible. And he continues to teach me to this day.

PRAY

When we were kids, we said our prayers every night before going to bed. Then we grew up. We became invincible young adults. We began to pray a little less, pushing our faith a little deeper in our hearts. After all, we knew everything.

Then life happened, and the clouds rolled in. We made poor choices, mistakes, and bad decisions. We lost people and things dear to us. *Prayer doesn't work, look at what happened.* And we buried our faith completely.

Then we became a little older, maybe wiser, and with few other options, we began to pray a little. Much to our surprise, even though we were beaten and bruised by life, the clouds parted, and the sun reappeared. Our faith began to push back to the surface.

Wait, maybe that was just me. There are those among us blessed to have maintained their faith along their life journey. Perhaps they were not tested as often as me, maybe they are just stronger. Sitting here with the benefit of experience, more than a few decades removed from those bedtime prayers, my spirit is renewed, and my faith has been restored. I don't wear my faith on my sleeve, there is little chance I will ever be an evangelist, but my faith is very deep and personal.

Today, I do not consider myself a religious man. I rarely quote scripture, but I am in touch with God on mutual terms. My relationship with God is personal, and prayer is once again part of my daily routine. My days begin and end with gratitude.

I respect all points of view on this, but to even begin to wrap ourselves around the human condition, we must believe in something bigger. Whatever that is to you, whatever he/she/it looks like, believe. I don't feel that I am born again, I feel that I have improved in faith. I was born and raised Catholic, and over time, became not a very good one. I look at this more like my "second helping of life."

When we are going about the business of living, so many things go unnoticed. Then, blessed by time, we look back, and life tells a much different story. Looking back, I still can't say with any certainty when I lost faith, but I know when I found it again. It was when I had finally run out of lies.

Over the course of our lives, when we have failed, when we have caused others harm, when we have been weak and wrong, the way we see life and death changes. And it changes our understanding of faith. Our connection to God becomes deeper. Where prayer once represented hope, it now represents acceptance, responsibility, accountability, and forgiveness. As a child, I prayed every day before bed. As a young man, I prayed in church. At the beginning of middle age, I did not pray. Now, at the end of middle age, I pray every day again, but for a different purpose.

How is prayer connected with living, loving, and learning? The first four pillars provide the electrical current that powers your inner light that illuminates the path ahead of you for everyone to follow. You can't be who you were meant to be without them.

Few people along my journey have had the significant impact that Tom St. Clair had in my life. But my spiritual journey is a different story. Tom's influence not only ignited my spirit and brought my calling to the forefront, but he also fueled the passion that ultimately made me the man of faith that I am today. I met Tom when I was a confused Catholic with a wife and three children—at that time, I did not understand my life. Tom became pastor of the Belle Vernon First United Methodist Church, the church my ex-wife grew up in, and a church that was completely foreign to me.

At that point in my life, every single day was a fistfight with myself, who I was, and who I thought I should be. Even though I was young and strong, those demons had already become more than I could carry. I was angry with myself and lost the core of my essence. My heart was gone, and in its place was a dark, seemingly bottomless pit that nothing could fill. Rev. St. Clair opened a door that I had previously been afraid to walk through. But he gave me the confidence to walk through it and embrace what lay ahead.

My spiritual journey hasn't been easy. The lingering beliefs of my youth have been difficult to shake.

It was Tom St. Clair who taught me how to pray. Growing up Catholic in the 1960s and 1970s in western Pennsylvania, an area steeped in tradition, the pomp and circumstance of the traditional Catholic Mass was all that I knew. Prayer was a chore, a task you were required to do. Tom showed me the connection of prayer to the heart. It became a choice rather than a chore, something I started looking forward to. It was then that prayer became part of my morning routine.

The first Sunday service that I attended at the Belle Vernon First UMC, I met Rev. St. Clair. I remember that first service like it was yesterday. There was this informal free-flowing service led by an open, affable, and completely approachable leader who engaged everyone in the building. Especially that confused young father searching for himself. When that light hit my heart, it started the change.

My confusion must have been palpable at that first meeting because Tom pulled me aside, and we had the first of many spiritual conversations. Our talks lifted my soul and brought my life into alignment for the first time. Those demons were too strong, and I destroyed that marriage and pretty much burned that life to the ground. It was Rev. St. Clair who showed me that God loves a sinner. Even though we didn't talk regularly after he moved from Belle Vernon, whenever I reached out, he answered. He sat in my chair and talked me through more than one crisis of the soul.

Tom St. Clair became a great friend, a leader I hold in the highest regard, and the most important spiritual mentor of my life. Tom left us in 2021 at the far too young age of 70. But my faith is strong because of him, and those talks live on in my heart.

Just a Conversation

I do not believe that God judges us on how or where we worship. Our connection to him is within ourselves, and he meets us where we are. Sometimes people prefer to gather more officially in his house, while on other occasions or for other people, we prefer to grab a cup of coffee with him on our own.

I used to pray in the darkness of scarcity and fear. That was before I realized that you gain strength, courage, and confidence through every experience in which you stop to look fear straight in the eye and do the thing you think you can't possibly do. It's a selfless act that inspires others to do the same.

It takes strength to lift others. It takes courage to go first. It takes confidence to stand alone. I find my strength, courage, and confidence in prayer, so by doing it every day, I don't need to do it out of fear anymore.

It's just a conversation between God and me.

It helps me be the leader I want to be. Now. Today. In the moment. The true value of a leader is not measured by the work they do. The true value of a leader is measured by the work they inspire others to do. My inspiration comes from my prayer time. That's when God sits in my chair.

Before my father passed, I spent some time with him. While Doodles was sleeping, I decided to go for a walk. I kept looking at the mountain across from their place and for some reason decided I had to climb it. Now going from a casual walk to literally climbing a mountain is not the best plan that I've ever had. But for some reason I was compelled to do it, I can't honestly explain it. There are several well-worn paths up this particular little mountain. However, not one of them called to me. I knew I had to make my own path.

I thought I had to prove to myself that I could climb a mountain without him. That may sound crazy, even a bit dramatic, but it's the truth. Because in life there will always be another mountain. But that wasn't it at all. About halfway up, I started questioning my judgment. Making my own path was much more difficult than I anticipated. But something ... someone kept compelling me forward.

He was showing me we are both ready for what is next.

Not knowing what I would find at the top, or even what I hoped to find, I knew one thing for certain: under no circumstances could I give up and turn back.

I honestly can't explain what I felt standing at the top of this little mountain; though my heart was breaking, my spirits were soaring. I felt lighter than I think I ever have in my life. The clarity of purpose is a bit overwhelming. All I can say, when I looked out over the Yucaipa Valley, a place I had no previous connection to, except that at that moment, I realized it was the place where my father's journey would soon end. But there was peace.

We often find God within ourselves, but we also find him in the most breathtaking places in the world. In moments where we find ourselves in nature and in awe, that's when we discover the most profound truths about life, and yes, death. In the silence, in the stillness, we feel him move through us, and we feel part of something bigger than ourselves.

Mindfulness

I've found that prayer makes me more mindful. It makes me pause. It helps me ask the important questions and focus. That's how I got back on my path to who I want to be.

Who are you when you're not really you? The road to your best self can be a lonely place. There are many twists and turns, and even the most successful among us lose their way at some point. I've taken my share of wrong turns on this road and been lost many times. Call it what you will—obstacles, challenges, barriers, bumps in the road—adversity has many names and takes many shapes. It seems that although we may be prepared, it still hits us hard every time.

I know what it's like to look for happiness in all the wrong places. I know the pain of coming up empty, time after time. This led to my depression. I could not shake it. In fact, I still haven't, but now I am able to manage it.

My struggle with depression gave me cause to ask myself many questions. Some were existential, like "What is real?" Well, real is obvious, as evidenced by where my mind was then. Real is raw, it's messy, it's broken, and ultimately it is the truth. I watch broken people own their truth every day. People who have used their mess as their message. I listen and see them change.

These days, I speak my truth. I own my mess. I'm still a work in progress … always will be. There are still days, fewer and farther between, where the sky is gray, the rain refuses to cease, it's unrelenting, stinging my skin, and the wind just bites through my bones.

I'm not talking about the weather.

Depression caught me totally off guard. I had let others inside my head and became distracted from what was important. I became distracted from me. I didn't see depression coming, and by the time I did, I was in deep depression. It is painful … it wears on you. I have heard depression described as "death by a thousand paper cuts." That is about as accurate a description as I can give. It is debilitating. It stole years from my life.

"Talk to someone," they said. I did; nobody listened. At least, it seemed like nobody listened. Because my mind was too full and constantly wandering. Someone randomly suggested mindfulness practice, so with nothing left to lose, I tried it. I started reading and learned about meditation.

The Person in the Chair

You might be wondering why I'm talking about meditation in a chapter about prayer. They seem to be pretty different. Here's the thing, though: they balance each other out perfectly. Prayer is a conversation with God. Meditation is a conversation with our highest and best selves. If you're talking to God, you probably want to get on your path to being your highest and best self. Meditation helps you meet in the middle.

It was through this mindfulness practice, this meditation, that I found my way back to God. How's that for a circuitous path? A young man, born and raised in the Catholic Church gets lost and after years of wandering in the wilderness, finds his way home through a Buddhist practice. It is absolutely true. Sitting quietly with my thoughts on the cold, hard surface of rock bottom, I finally found peace. In that moment I finally understood God's plan for me. I now know that His plan for me is real. It was meditation that relaxed my mind and led me back to prayer.

In my quiet time, alone with my thoughts, I started asking myself the same question, "How do you climb Mt. Everest?" The answer? One step at a time. We know that Mt. Everest is the highest peak on earth, literally the top of the world. Very few humans have or will ever make that climb. It's possibly the greatest test of strength, stamina, physical skill, and human will, we can endure. Of course, you can fly over it in a jet, but it's not the same.

We have mountains to climb, physically and mentally, in our daily lives. We climb to the top of one mountain, only to see the next peak, and the one after that, and what becomes a seemingly endless mountain range. We naturally think the next mountain is too high and can't imagine how we're going to get over it.

One step at a time. It doesn't matter whether your step is an inch or a mile—as long as it is a step forward, you are making progress. What if we stumble? Fall? Get tired? Forget the path? The answer to all of this is mindfulness, mastering our thoughts. Through God, through prayer, through our connection to our best selves.

Let's show our children and grandchildren that the journey is everything. Every mountain, every step will bring them closer to who they are. When they climb together, respect each other, and accept each other's differences, they will fly above and over any mountain.

The question of how to climb Mt. Everest turned out to be a powerful one, which ignited a rebirth in my life. However, the most powerful question, and perhaps the most painful, was still to be answered. When the storm was raging at its loudest, the question always came. *Who am I?* When those days appeared, anger and ego, my two greatest nemeses, usually showed up. My first instinct was to retreat to something warm and familiar.

But I reached a point where I couldn't find anywhere to retreat: Everything and everyone was gone. As I sat on rock bottom, looking for a friendly face, a helping hand, a lifeline from anyone, I found nothing. In that moment of clarity came the realization that I was not actually sitting on rock bottom, but rather I was sitting on the foundation of which I could build my life.

And I wasn't alone.

I believe God put mindfulness practice in my life to give me the clarity to answer the question that was haunting me. *Who am I?* That is why I thank Him every day for the path he's set for me, my past, and the lessons that brought me to this day. That forward movement, that growth, is too valuable to let slip away.

Life is a journey with only one destination. Once you own your mess and speak your truth, your journey, even with the storms that show up along the way, becomes filled with blue skies and sunshine. It's in those real moments, the moments of adversity, that we are most vulnerable. We lose ourselves. How often have you said something or acted in a way when you were stressed that you've regretted? We rationalize. How many times have you said, or heard someone say, "Everything happens for a reason"? We blame. How often have you looked outward for reasons when things don't go your way?

There is purpose in every moment of adversity. Our first instinct tends to be to hide or run from adversity. But it's always best to face any obstacle head on. Because the quicker you figure out what that purpose is, the quicker you will use it to grow. Every adversity of mine has been a catalyst for future success. Of course, I can see this with the benefit of hindsight, but it's hard to wrap your head around it when you're in the middle of it. That doesn't make it any less true. There have been times when I've looked in the mirror and not recognized the person looking back at me. Those were the times when I lied, was judgmental, intolerant, unforgiving or just didn't do things the right way. I understand that I have failed ... many times. I am grateful for every obstacle of mine because they are lifting me closer to where I want to be.

In the pursuit of your best, your failures are the foundation on which you build "you." Where do you go to find "you" when you feel lost? You go within yourself. You see, that is where you are. And so is God. Meditation is a part of mindfulness and is the way you communicate within yourself. It teaches you to focus. Mindset training requires being present and paying full attention to the present moment. When we focus on the present moment, we become aware of our negative thoughts and acknowledge them without judgment.

Mindfulness tools, such as meditation, are easy to incorporate into your daily routine. Set aside 10 to 15 minutes to be still. Sit in a comfortable position and just breathe. It's as easy as breathing, something you have been doing your entire life. You should be pretty good at that.

If a thought floats in, refocus on your breath. You can do this.

And when you wrap up your meditation, this is an excellent prayer to connect your goals with God: "God, put the people in front of me I need to meet. Give voice to the words I need to speak." This is the "Lighthouse Prayer."

I love to start my day with this simple prayer. It can be life-changing. It opens your mind and heart to hold space for others. After years of being adrift at sea, I found myself in service. After years of being afraid of living, I found strength in service. At the end of our lives, all our material possessions, the money, the social media "likes," and all the accolades will matter very little compared to the legacy we leave behind.

Rather than living your life with worry and scarcity, why not choose to live a life of abundance and clarity?

It's OK if you can't see the path. Look for the lighthouse. Ask for help. Invite someone to sit in your chair. Taking that one step this week builds momentum so next week you take two steps. Find the lighthouse, and you'll never waste another moment of your precious life worrying about what others think. You will focus on growing yourself, so you can help others. You will become a lighthouse. Success will come to you based upon the way you treat others and how they feel about themselves after being with you.

The Lighthouse Prayer made a big difference in my life, in the middle of a lot of realizations about who I am and where I'm going. It was not until I made prayer and meditation part of my daily routine that my life became abundant.

Your spiritual relationship with God is not to be learned, but to be felt. Spiritual growth is deeply personal and individual. Be brave enough to seek God with the same passion as He seeks your heart.

My father grew up in the Catholic Church, but he was not a religious man. I don't ever remember seeing him pray. He was, however, deeply spiritual. He never walked away from the church, but he studied to learn the essential elements and traditions of other religions.

The journey with Christ is one of transformation. Our path to faith varies based on our life experiences. My father's journey was vastly different than mine, yet he tried to make me follow his path. He believed that it's about the process of getting there, not the arrival.

I have always seen myself as getting there ... a work in progress. But for years I had been walking followed closely by the shadow of a life unlived.

When I started my walk with Christ, a million pieces were scattered around my feet. As my journey unfolded, those pieces came together. While I'm not there yet, I'm walking in the right direction.

INSPIRE

Leadership is about inspiring people with hope, and hope is what second chances are all about. Think about all the people who have sat in your chair in your life. What did they give you? What made them leaders? I guarantee that after a good talk with any of them, you would have more hope than you did before. For me, that hope really did give me a second chance, especially in the darker times in my life. Hope was dwindling, but I was inspired and hopeful after a chat with the leader in my chair.

Inspire is the fifth pillar because you must be aligned with the first four to be able to do it. You must align your heart and life with your mission, which means learning and praying to be on the correct path. Once you have all of that, my friend, you can inspire and give hope with your actions.

To inspire, in my mind, is to live in such a way that your life's message is so powerful that it becomes your legacy without you intending it to be. Nobody will ever duplicate the inspirational majesty of the Sistine Chapel. Yet, Michelangelo never intended to create an inspirational piece that would become one of the major artistic accomplishments of human civilization and inspire millions for over 500 years. Pieces like the Sistine Chapel ceiling became his legacy because he aligned with who he was meant to be and painted from the heart.

Inspiration should always come from the heart and be firmly rooted in truth. True inspiration is something that cannot be forced; it must come naturally. One can inspire with words and actions, but the most impactful inspiration is not seen or heard; it is felt and lived.

Growing up, I didn't have to look far for inspiration. I was blessed to be one of the hundreds of kids my father inspired as a teacher at Charleroi High School in Pennsylvania. The poem "Shifting the Sun"[2] opens with, "When your father dies, say the Irish / you lose your umbrella against bad weather." I know that I'm not the only one who has lost their father. But I've learned the truth in that poem ... when your father dies, your loss is unique, profound, and yours alone. Even though we had deeply personal and profound conversations in the weeks before he died, I think every day of all the things I meant to say, to ask, and the things I still need to learn from him.

A few years ago, Terrilynn and I attended a family reunion with my parents. A distinguished and soft-spoken gentleman around my father's age introduced himself as "Robert Abbott." I had only heard stories about him from my father, so I knew he was an accomplished athlete and a good man. He asked if he could tell me a story, and we stepped aside from the crowd.

It turns out that he was a few years younger than my dad and played on his high school's 1959 undefeated championship football team. My father was a member of the coaching staff, even though football wasn't his game. Doodles was a basketball guy. His biggest contribution to that team was just being there and being who he is: an inspiration.

The story I was told that day was powerful, so much so that as he was telling it, this gentleman teared up and began to cry. He went on to tell me that he had a great season as a junior in 1958, the year before they won the championship, being recruited by several colleges. But during that special season, he was hurt most of the time and felt that he let his teammates

---

[2] "Shifting the Sun" by Diana Der-Hovanessian, from *Selected Poems.* © Sheep Meadow Press, 1994.

down. Rather than joining in with his teammates to enjoy the excitement of the trip to Pittsburgh to play in that championship game ... he sat quietly by himself.

Mr. Abbott proceeded to tell me that my father sat down beside him and spoke quietly to only him. He wouldn't tell me everything that he said on that bus ride, but what stood out to him was that my father told him he knew he would do something in this game to help his team win. Mr. Abbott explained that at the time he thought my father was just trying to get him motivated to play.

Well wouldn't you know that in that championship game, Bobby Abbott scooped up a fumble and raced 58 yards for a touchdown, securing a 13-12 victory. He then pulled out his wallet and showed me a worn and faded piece of paper. On it was written the rest of what my father had told him over 50 years ago.

We will likely never know exactly what he said to Bobby Abbott on that bus, but it was powerful enough to inspire that young man for a lifetime.

Seek what they Sought

Matsuo Basho, a 17th-century Japanese haiku master, wrote, "Do not follow in the footsteps of others. Instead, seek what they sought." My father was very successful in his life, and he taught me many valuable lessons. One thing he never wanted me to do is follow in his footsteps. Everything we talked about, every lesson, was to help me find my own path. And once I was on that path, I knew that it was up to me to leave a legacy for others to seek what I sought. But I never considered myself to be a particularly inspirational person. So I was surprised when my good friend Mary Dreliszak wrote her book, *People Who Inspire,* and included me.

That was the first time I ever considered that I *could* be inspirational. Since then, I have studied, researched, and sought out inspirational people because it made me realize that I liked the idea of inspiring people. And I knew that the type of people who inspire me are the type of people I also aspire to be.

They are idealists. They are optimists. They overestimate what we are capable of and inspire us to see what they see and believe it.

That's when I started writing social media posts about what I learned, how it spun in my brain. I joined the conversation. Then something strange happened: people responded. I started writing more, blogging, and contributing a column to my local newspaper.

When I think about the people in my life who inspire me, my father is at the top of the list. He was a naturally inspirational guy, and he inspired me to love life. It would have been easy to follow in his footsteps, but then I would not have walked the path that led me here. I would not have risen above the adversity that shaped me. I would not be who I am.

Every morning, for well over ten years, just before I walk out the door to begin my day, I say the Lighthouse Prayer, which I mentioned in the last chapter. "God, put the people in front of me I need to meet. Give voice to the words I need to speak." That is our opportunity to have an impact, to inspire, to make a difference.

If our presence doesn't make an impact, our absence won't make a difference.

In today's world, it's easy to become full of ourselves. We have a little success, maybe make some money and suddenly we're "special." We seek the accolades that our society bestows on the famous. Our society rewards the popular, the things that are trendy ... but not necessarily the things that make a difference.

Inspiring people are usually ordinary people stepping up and doing extraordinary things.

When we inspire, we share a message so powerful that it becomes our legacy. Legacy isn't flashy or sexy. Legacy is gritty, covered in sweat, maybe a drop or two of blood ... and certainly more tears than can be captured. Legacy is, above all else, impactful.

I've asked myself this many times: What would happen if I left social media and stopped writing my blog? How many of my 5,000 friends would miss it? How many would miss me? Would anyone remember the message? Live it or share it?

My answer reminds me of why I started it in the first place.

We spend a considerable amount of time vying for attention. We all want validation, but we must be willing to put in the work that inspires others to be worthy of their attention.

You may never know for sure who is watching or how you are impacting someone's life. You may never know who you are inspiring.

But our legacy matters. What we do matters. Do what you love and inspire others to do the same.

When you show up prepared every day, and do what you say you're going to do, have faith that your work will inspire others ... that's how you make a difference.

Your Truth

Every single day, people lead and inspire. They go about the business of living in such a way that we take notice. There is one thing that separates a true leader from a mere pretender: truth.

Truth is not something you can hear; you must see and feel it. Because of their words, we take notice of certain people and are compelled to look deeper. The purest form of truth, unedited by our brains, comes from the gut.

If the truth comes from within us, why can it be so difficult to find? The world is full of people trying to advise us, persuade us, analyze us, and judge us. All of this is noise that just causes confusion and dilutes the truth. With all these distractions, how are we supposed to hear our own inner voice speaking our own unique truth?

It's hard to ignore the clutter and live our truth with commitment and conviction. When we commit to being completely truthful—and that can manifest in several ways—we commit to being a better person and making the world around us a better place. To change what's negative in our lives to positive and grow as a person, we must first and foremost be truthful with ourselves, accept and embrace our inner truth, even if we don't like what it says about us, and express it through our actions.

The most genuine leaders I have ever witnessed or read about in history books did not tell people what to do; they showed them. They understood that, to create a movement, people had to believe in them, not just their words.

Great leaders know when it is time to give ownership of a movement to their followers and become a follower as well.

Truth Leads to Purpose

What is the meaning of life? Why are we here? What is our purpose? For as long as there has been human life, we have had questions about our existence. These questions, though seemingly simple, have answers that lead to more questions. But in the journey lies the real answers. In the action. Inspiration and purpose go hand in hand because those who are so enveloped in their purpose that they follow their path unwaveringly are the ones who inspire without even trying.

Finding purpose is not easy, in fact, you may go an entire lifetime without finding it. Not everyone believes they have a purpose, but not believing won't keep you from discovering it, just as not believing in gravity won't keep you from tripping.

How does an average human discover their purpose in life? Start with yourself. Live intentionally, always being open to all things and honest with yourself. Wake up every morning *on purpose*. Seek where your passion lives and choose to go there often. That is where the beautiful, passionate soul within you is waiting for you to find them.

Make making a difference your priority. Show up and make it happen. It takes action. You only have this one cosmic moment to do everything you will ever do, so don't hesitate. Make a life to be proud of. Kiss deeply, laugh often, love faithfully, and speak truthfully. Do what makes you happy every day. Make someone smile. You can make beautiful things happen. Color outside the lines, outkick your coverage, go beyond what you believe are your limits.

Your purpose is waiting beyond your comfort zone.

Purpose really comes down to only three questions you need ask yourself:

1. Did I love enough?
2. Did I laugh enough?
3. Did I make a difference?

When the answer to all three is "yes," you will have found your purpose.

Purpose matters. A sense of purpose establishes our mindset. Purpose is directly linked to optimism, it's our inward motivation, it's why we do what we do. Our purpose doesn't have to be a big splash. It can be that little thing that drives us through the negative clutter and pushes us forward.

With purpose, our dreams become goals, and our goals become reality. It's how we know what needs to be done. It's what stops us from talking about it and leads us to be about it.

Our purpose allows us to inspire others. Inspiring and connecting people leads to innovative and collaborative thinking. We are most inspiring when we share our faults and failures honestly and rise above them. Showing people that it's OK to fail opens people up to exploring new ideas because they realize that they, too, can try new things and fail, and don't have to be perfect. This is what leading, inspiring, and motivating people is about!

Being inspirational requires you to be seen; you must open yourself to scrutiny and intentionally become vulnerable. I never hide from my failures. In fact, I revisit them regularly to remind myself of where I came from and to never lose sight of where I am going. Every mistake, every adversity that distracted me from my purpose, every obstacle on my journey that tripped me up has made me the man I am today.

When I was in the throes of divorce, bankruptcy, and depression ... there was a silver lining. I was hired for the best job and the most money of my career. It was a blessing. It was the beginning of my life after divorce ... my new life. Unfortunately, I didn't appreciate it, and wasn't ready for it. I was successful, but the actions and habits that led to the divorce continued. And ultimately, I crashed.

I was the only person surprised when I was fired from that job. Telling Terrilynn what happened was the hardest conversation of my life. But it was one of the most revealing to me. Things that I had tucked away in the deep recesses of my brain suddenly had to be faced.

It was about that time when I began journaling. It's funny how the truth just flows out of the tip of that pen. The success found in that job was lost because I wasn't grateful for the opportunity. Gratitude was found in the humility of loss.

Although you can't go back and create a new beginning, you can begin today to create a new ending.

Nobody will care what you do, or how you do it, until they understand why you're doing it. You must win hearts before minds. It's not about making money. That is a result. Your "why" is deeper. It's your very reason for being. It's the foundation that your purpose in life is built upon. It's who you are.

Efforts today rarely produce results today, though. Success in life, just like any worthwhile endeavor, takes consistent effort day in and day out over a long period of time. There is a Greek Proverb that pretty much defines how I live: "A society grows when old men plant trees whose shade they will never sit in." My greatest hope is that your children and mine, our grandchildren, and their children, will have plenty of shade long after I'm gone. Be patient, plant your tree, and let it grow for generations to come.

There is no more beautiful tree than the tree of legacy.

No matter where you have been, no matter what you're going through, you have the power to create the future you desire. Think about it. Take a moment to reflect on how good life really is. Think about the path you've traveled to get here. Yes, we have a long way to go. We still have much to learn about loving each other. We still must silence the noise that distracts us from that unconditional love of humanity. But, we're making forward progress on our journey. Our destination is barely visible on the horizon. Yet, there is hope that we are getting closer.

In life, some doors will close, and others will open. There's a reason: as you level up in life, you will constantly transform into newer and better versions of you. You must close some doors behind you and not try to reopen them. Just trust and move on to the next open door. Live your life on your terms. I hold myself to a high standard; sometimes it's difficult to hit the target. But, I set the standard, and it was set that high for a reason. The world around us changes for the better when we change ourselves for the better.

Change the World

Purpose is bigger than just us. Connect your heart to a bigger purpose, a bigger vision to change the world. Start there to inspire. I know, lots of people run around shouting they're going to "change the world!" and far too few of them follow through. The excitement wears off, and the reality of the work necessary quells any remaining enthusiasm. Believing that you can make your life, as well as the lives of the people around you better, is the beginning of success. No matter what you do in life, success starts right there. Commitment to that belief will determine whether you will ultimately succeed or fail.

When we simply do what we believe and put it to purposeful action, people will follow. That's leadership: having a vision of the future, believing, going there, and doing what you believe. I'm often asked how I stay so positive all the time. I don't. I don't wake up inspired every morning. I get beat down by the business of life just like everyone else. There is always resistance, always another obstacle. Our unwavering commitment is what pushes past the resistance and smashes through obstacles, keeping us on the right path.

The challenge of our future is much more exciting than anything we are doing or have done. It's unknown, there is risk, but there is also hope. Let's change the world.

The little things in life tell the real story. Love comes from the little things. Joy comes from celebrating the little things. Peace is hidden amongst the little things. Life is the accumulation of the little things that come and go every day almost unnoticed, inspiring us to be greater than we already are.

Your impact from living a life, your legacy, doesn't come from a big splash. It comes from the ripples spreading across the water.

There was one thing that Doodles had no patience for, and that was quitting. Unfortunately, quitting was something I became very good at. When I was in the dark, I quit more times than I can count. But the last time I was faced with that choice was the most significant because, if I had chosen to quit that time, there would be no turning back. If I had quit that day, my life would end.

When Olivia Behanna Saved my Life

I was introduced to Olivia Behanna several years ago by Terrilynn, whose sister had a dance studio. Two of our granddaughters had dance classes there. Now, dance recitals were never one of my favorite things, but that year was different. That year I met one of the most inspirational people I have ever known. Terrilynn nudged me to ensure I was paying attention and told me I wouldn't want to miss the next dancer. The curtain opened, and Olivia stood with her back to the audience while we listened to her powerful words, words so innocent and strong.

She told the story of her experience with cancer in her own words, which touched me deeply that evening. I had given up hope. I was at a tipping point in my life and could have easily slid back down the mountain I had climbed. But Olivia unknowingly propelled me forward. She inspired me to keep climbing. At the time, I was acquainted with her parents but didn't know them well. I met her mother and asked if I could talk to Olivia. She was the sweetest kid, yet she had a presence. Olivia was blessed with a beautiful gift and shared it with me that evening. Her gift was inspiration. She was strong and vulnerable in a way I had never seen before. Her story went straight to my heart. If this young woman had the courage to go on that stage alone and share her story ... then I could too.

PART II
BUILDING ON THE PILLARS

Of course, the five pillars are the foundational piece of leadership, but the other pieces of the puzzle build on them. Once your pillars are in place, you'll be able to grow and sit in others' chairs to lead and inspire.

CREATIVE MORNINGS

My chair is showing visible signs of wear. It's been repaired many times, is threadbare in spots and has more than a few scratches. But it's beautiful. The wear results from the time spent in that chair by my father and some of the most amazing people I've ever known. Along my journey, there have been many occupants in that old chair. All have refined it with hand-hewn wisdom, with some adding new things and others taking old things away. That's how my old chair has taken shape over the years.

When it comes to who you allow to sit in your chair, be cautious—and even more so when it comes to whose chair you choose to sit in. You'll never accomplish anything alone; success only happens when you surround yourself with great people. So look for the ones who give you space to live your life yet stay close enough to guide you when it gets dark. Love yourself so you understand how to love them. Learn from them. Stand with the ones who pray in the good times, not only the bad.

They don't belong in your chair if they don't inspire you.

The seeds of Live. Love. Learn. Pray. Inspire. were planted during childhood. But they didn't bloom until I nurtured them in the creative mornings of adulthood. There is a beautiful stillness in the early morning. We all know life has ugly parts, and you can't just wish them pretty. You can, however, make your life beautiful simply by choosing to love it.

When I was a young man, the world's expectation of me was that I would fail. I was widely perceived as selfish and maybe a bit arrogant. In my heart, none of that was true. But back then, I wasn't living in my heart. So... I lied. Of course, nobody believed the lies but me.

Perception is reality; back then, I couldn't escape the reality I had created. The chaos overwhelmed me. The noise only made me angry. I became someone impossible to be proud of. But in the stillness, I learned that failure has its place. Once the anger in your face dies down... you're left with the truth. Not just any truth, but "the truth." And within the truth, you'll find peace. Now my words are true, speaking from experience, by a man who has known heartbreaking pain and conquered it. I stopped blaming others for all my failures and started working to clean up my mess. And what a mess it was.

You can craft a life of stillness, peace, and truth when you embrace your heart. That simple acceptance makes all the difference.

We fear failure because it's loud and happens in the spotlight, while success is quietly earned alone in the dark. That's stillness. Allow yourself to learn the lesson. Not everyone will get you, and that's OK. Allow yourself space to be rejected. That's peace. I share my story because I spent a long time chasing something that wasn't meant for me. I was hiding from the truth. Living a lie takes a lot of energy, and it never ends well. In my story, it lured me down the rabbit hole of depression. From there, becoming the villain in my own story was easy.

Now I speak the truth quickly... it's right there for everyone to see; no more lying to myself. That's the truth. Stillness, peace, and truth are earned in the trenches.

That's why I visit the worst moments of my life rather than avoid them. I own them and the demons I created there. It's up to me to ensure that's where they stay. There's no more fanning the flames of failure by blaming others. There's only facing the truth and winning. In the early morning, I learned to appreciate a great cup of coffee. Suddenly, I started noticing ordinary, everyday things differently. When I chose not to settle for the ordinary, I learned that the best cup of coffee is even better when accompanied by a great conversation.

Life finally got my attention. Every single sunrise has become extraordinary, and I know that a child's laugh can be held in your heart forever. I have a sense of purpose. The smell of fresh bread right out of the oven is hearing the words, "I love you." Those are just a few of the simple, everyday things that I love... things that once went mostly unnoticed in the selfish busyness of my life. Things that have enriched my life simply because I started paying attention.

All of it means something. Life is mostly ordinary... so much so that we miss most of it. But those ordinary sights, sounds, smells, and tastes make living it extraordinary. There are so many things that can go wrong in our lives. There will always be obstacles to overcome... bumps in the road we travel. None of them can diminish the beauty of the journey we share. We must allow ourselves to feel all of it and let the journey be our teacher. Everything in life can be beautiful if we choose to see it. We're blessed to have that choice. If you're hurting, I'll see you. I'm here for you. I choose to offer my heart to ease your pain.

Doodles always said, "Don't be focused on the splash, or you'll miss the ripple. The most beautiful things live in the ripples." Every time our hearts touch, we send a ripple that changes everything around us. There's nothing that compares to the mixing of human hearts. We must show up for each other when it's inconvenient or cold or dark. We can't hide inside ourselves when the person next to us is in the storm. No one has to carry that weight alone. We all can show up for each other with kindness, love, grace, patience, and compassion.

We humans love to judge others, mainly to feel better about ourselves. I've had my share of judgments from the many critics in my life. But somehow, they're all gone. No... they're still there, but I don't hear them anymore. No one has ever walked around in my skin but me. Nobody has seen the world through my eyes but me. For years I failed to be honest... I lied to myself and everyone around me. I was uncomfortable in the skin I was in. Because there was always the need for others to accept me. I became the person those judges in the cheap seats wanted me to be... and failed to be true to myself.

I believed them and became the poster child for not being good enough. All it did was lead to a life filled with anger and frustration nearly 24/7. I wasn't a pleasant person to be around. First, it punched me in the gut, but ultimately, that anger knocked me down... and out. I'm telling you this standing here after many years of being anger free. There was to be no more tapping, no nudging. That knockout punch is how life got my attention...

I used to think that being accepted by others... especially the cool kids... was going to make me happy and give me the fulfillment I had hoped for. Truthfully, though, it never did. It's taken me some time to get it right, but I finally love the skin I'm in. You don't have to wait for your life to turn upside down like I did to know you're good enough. Accept all of you and understand that every situation, every experience, and every person in your life was meant to be there—even the bad ones.

Embracing who you are right here, right now, redefines "good enough." Make a conscious decision right now to love yourself, trust yourself, and not care what others think. Be you, for you. Whoever doesn't accept that doesn't belong with you. Love the skin you're in, no matter how wrinkled or scarred. It's your life... live it your way. Confucius said, at least the Internet says Confucius said, "We have two lives, and the second begins when we realize we only have one."

I read that last night, and it was still on my heart this morning. You may never find that perfect fit. Let go of the life you had planned, so you can love the life you have. Be present in this life... the one you're living. Lead with love in everything you do, and connect authentically with everyone you meet.

We start out on this journey seeking our perfect life, and then along the way, we encounter many obstacles, we're judged and criticized... so we wander off on a few detours. We course-correct several times... and ultimately we end up living the life that we're meant to live.

I had to hit rock bottom a couple of times in my life, mentally, financially, and spiritually to understand that the life I was chasing simply wasn't meant for me. Those times tested my faith and made me question every decision I've ever made. I finally had no choice but to face my truth. A new friend said to me just yesterday, "Your light shines brightest in the dark." Looking back, I'm grateful for the lessons that showed me that the life I'm living fits me perfectly. Letting go of what I thought I wanted allowed me to start the journey within. That's where I found the life meant for me.

When you find yourself sitting there with your life turned upside down, you're as raw as you'll ever be. Every minute detail swells your heart with humility and grace... and your second life begins. I'm grateful for that dark time that forced me to see myself truthfully and appreciate the beautiful blessing of the one life I get to live.

It's from there on the bottom looking up at my life that my journey truly began.

Wherever you are in life, regardless if you're in pain or struggling... let it go. Know that you are exactly where you're supposed to be. Make this your "bottom moment" and start here. Look into your heart. What you'll find there is the core of the life you seek. You'll fall in love with the life you're already living there.

I'm quick to smile these days. Presence pulls the strings on my smile each morning. I've been blessed with another day. But look behind the smile... do you see it? Yes, I'm broken. I battle depression every day, because every day I'm afraid that this may be the day it will win. "But you're always so positive and you seem so happy." I get that a lot. Some just don't get it. That's why I share my story... that's why I write about it. That's why I live with gratitude, love, grace, kindness, and compassion. Because I've seen the darkness... and I know I'm not alone.

I want others to know they aren't alone by reading my words. Want to do the same for the next guy? There is absolutely nothing so powerful as a simple hand-written note. When I was at my worst... when the most important people in my life became strangers nearly overnight, someone shared powerful words with me. Reading those words, I can easily see that they were written with a shaking hand. But those scribbled words changed my life. I remember reading that note like it was yesterday. I think about the words on that tear-stained page every day. In those words, I found peace, and my heart began to heal. They were the most powerful words I've ever read.

Nothing I have written since even comes close. Yes... I wrote those words in a note to myself, sitting alone in the pitch dark on the worst day of my life. It was the first entry in my first journal. The reason that simple note written in a journal 20 years ago is so profoundly important to me is that it led me to truth, acceptance, and accountability. That note is the reason why I chose this path... to make a difference in the lives of others before all else. To ensure that the people I meet on this journey will be better because I came through this way.

Write your own words so honestly and raw that they jump off the page and wrap themselves around your heart. In your own words, you can change your life. Regardless of what you accomplish on this journey... in the end, all you will have left is you.

VULNERABILITY

Vulnerability is the new black. Everybody is talking about it. Everybody wants it. Can you get a package of it at Target? Amazon? Probably not, but vulnerability definitely has a five-star rating in my book.

Being vulnerable in our society today is nothing short of a superpower.

What it is: Letting yourself be seen from an empowered standpoint. You've overcome obstacles, and now you're ready to share the truth about them.

What it isn't: Spilling your secrets all over the place without rhyme or reason. It shouldn't sound like ranting, whining, or complaining.

And that can be a tough balance to strike.

If you feel fear about being seen and putting your life out in the open, don't worry ... this is *normal*. Nobody wants to be judged. In fact, being seen is perhaps the most unnatural thing we can imagine.

The five pillars expose your vulnerability. We are not alone. There are others struggling with what we have overcome. That is why we must share our experiences with people who need to hear them.

Vulnerability is unnerving, but when you have faith in yourself and your message is coming from the purest place of truth, your heart, you have nothing to fear. If people cannot see you, the real you, they will not be able to find the path to your heart.

I remember Doodles telling me how his life was saved as a young man. Everyone he knew was in his head telling him to become a pharmacist. His head led him to Duquesne University, where he was miserable. One conversation put him in touch with his heart, and he let his passion pull him to California State Teachers College and the two passions in his life (other than Saundra): teaching and basketball. The rest, as they say, is history.

I inherited his passion for basketball at an early age but wasn't blessed with that one conversation until I was much older ... because, of course, I had to find out the hard way. But, once I surrendered to my passion, my life took a dramatic turn. My path forward became clear. I no longer had to seek my purpose; it found me. My purpose led me to an unlikely place, one that a few years before I would never have imagined was mine. Look in your heart, be vulnerable, take a deep dive, and have that one conversation. You will learn amazing things about yourself.

Sharing my Failure

I've stood alone, lost and broken, accused of and judged for things that I've said and done. Some of it exaggerated, some of it just false ... most of it true.

I wear the scars openly ... uncovered for everyone to see. Because I'm accountable for all of it. I own it.

Being lost in plain sight is painful, especially when it's self-inflicted. I looked for validation all around me and found out the hard way that nothing coming from outside can fix what's happening inside. All I accomplished was to push my negative self-talk even deeper ... like a dagger to the heart. Unfortunately, my actions followed and betrayed my truth.

You never will know how many lives you can change until you are brave enough to be vulnerable and open your heart for everyone to see your pain. Being vulnerable is being brave. For far too long, I was afraid. I tried to hide my stumbles, mistakes, and failures. But they became too heavy. I learned the hard way to be comfortable in this discomfort.

There are some failures we must own because to deny them causes pain. For me, it started with an innocent conversation. I guess guilt or innocence is a matter of perspective. Regardless of the lens through which you happen to look, that conversation was the beginning of the end of my marriage. It started a 20-year story of marriage, divorce, emotional damage ... and a journey to find redemption, forgiveness, trust, and true love.

God gives us every opportunity to walk away from temptation but leaves it far too easy to choose to walk toward it. I was depressed, lost, and vulnerable. Temptation overwhelmed me. I gave in far too often, guaranteeing that my marriage would end, and every subsequent relationship would be at risk. Giving into temptation became habitual. My experience profoundly changed me and has changed my family dynamic forever.

We all must live with the consequences of our choices. I was blessed in that moment to find Terrilynn. When I needed someone who could see the man through the mess and love me ... there she was.

But some wrongs you just can't shake off. Even if they lead to many rights that benefit many others, they stay with you.

You can't fear failure; if you're living, it's inevitable, so don't hide from it, don't deny it. Rather, embrace it, share it, talk to someone about it, and do it better the next time. Never try to hide from mistakes. Face them in the moment and learn from them. Be accountable for the pain your actions inflicted on others. I share my divorce as an example because I hid from it.

I became angry and resentful over something that I ultimately caused. That anger and resentment stemmed from putting myself last and pushing through with a marriage that ultimately didn't make any of us happy. I thought I was putting myself last, at least, but in reality I was selfishly putting myself first. When I splashed that anger and resentment on everyone around me—even those I wanted to protect—I deflected responsibility away from myself.

My ex-wife and our children weren't the only ones hurt— Terrilynn was hurt too. Her children were in pain, as well, because of the actions I refused to own at that time. They say that time heals all wounds. That isn't true. The only way to heal those wounds is by being humble, vulnerable, and accountable. You have to own the pain you caused as much as the pain you felt. We are blessed with the ability to learn from and grow above our mistakes, to be vulnerable with ourselves, to dig into our truths, and plant new seeds. Divorce taught me to love more deeply, appreciate every breath, and be accountable for every word and action.

Each divorce is different because it impacts the people involved in unexpected ways. Everyone processes trauma in a very personal way. There's no right or wrong way, only your way. Where we go wrong is not respecting the needs of all involved. Divorce is loss, and like any loss, it must be grieved. Ours taught me that my choices should be thought through and filtered through my heart. If I had respected that my ex-wife needed to grieve the loss and given her the space to process the trauma ... perhaps we could have avoided some of the pain.

Through that experience, I learned how to love, and I've become a better man: stronger in faith, and character.

Holding Space

Vulnerability also means holding space for others. I lost my children in that divorce, not through a custody fight, but through my words and actions. My role as a father was forever damaged during that time. They see me differently, and between then and now, those relationships have gone from an up-and-down to nonexistent. I never really understood the word "estrangement" until it happened to us. I will always hold space for them just as I will always love them unconditionally and without judgment.

There is an emptiness inside me, and I've put my heart in the palm of God's hand and given up control.

Holding space isn't always romantic. But it is always human. It's how humans should interact with each other. It's a pleasant good morning to the stranger behind you in line at the cafe. It can be that ordinary. It means being present. When you hold space for someone, you open yourself and give the entirety of yourself to them.

You give them your presence for that moment in time. It's a beautiful gift, not from you, but *of* you, that they can carry away with them.

It means we all matter. Everyone wants to matter. We all want our lives to have meaning. We are imperfect souls living in an imperfect world. But freely giving just a moment of your imperfect self to another can take us all to a better place.

Holding space means honoring each person for who they are deep inside no matter what the outside looks like, no matter the mess, no matter the day or season. It means being human and allowing others to be human in our presence.

Built by Mistakes

We all should dream big, create a vision around our dreams, and set goals to make those dreams reality.

Everything starts with a dream. Even at my age, I'm still dreaming, still believing, and still working toward my dreams, because there is much left to do. I think about the future, where I want to go, and what I want to accomplish. In those moments, I stop to appreciate what I have now and realize how far I've come. Around 1977, I began my quest to set the World Record for making mistakes. It wasn't intentional, mind you, but that's when I set my feet on that path. I got really good at it. As the mistakes, poor choices, stumbles, and bad decisions piled up, my competition dwindled. Looking at the highlight reel from that time in my life, I realize that they were all pretty much my fault.

I thought I was walking the easy path, but all I was doing was refusing to grow up, become responsible and accountable for the man I was ... in other words, being an adult. Well, adulting was boring. So, I stayed the course, and kept making mistakes. But, through it all, something happened: I learned things. Next thing I knew, I grew up. And eventually, I became responsible too. Along the way, I lost a lot, but I gained experience, a bunch of bumps and bruises, and a few scars.

I learned how to be loved and to love myself. I also learned the true meaning of gratitude, humility, grace, clarity, peace— and most importantly, accountability.

Being vulnerable won't prevent life's ugly moments from happening. It just lessens their impact because we own what we have done and understand our role in creating our lives. So always keep your heart open and be grateful for the opportunities you're given along the way. I've known pain in my life. I dragged it around for years. It made me angry, hurtful, and miserable. I dragged it around with me because I laid it at the feet of others. I wasn't truthful with myself ... or anyone else for that matter. The moment I took responsibility, started to share, and let go was the moment I took my life back.

No matter who is to blame, you can't change it. Blame is easy. One of our most destructive human pastimes is playing the blame game. If something goes wrong in our lives, we can just throw up our hands and say, "Not my fault." In blaming others for our difficulties, we can pretend we're something we're not. We avoid our truth.

You can't control the circumstances into which you were born. You can't control the adversity that will most assuredly enter your life. You *can* control how you respond. You *can* control how you live your life. That will always be your choice. Always accept and embrace the truth. Be the truth.

Start by owning *you.*

Start loving your flaws, your awkwardness, your weirdness, and your vulnerability. Only when you accept everything you are and are not do you truly succeed in life. Put down your anger. Your life is a journey of transformation. You are exploring the wisdom of your soul, and the joy of your heart. Have faith, be courageous ... for you are becoming you.

When I was 39 years old, I literally blew up my life. I lost my family, and just about everything that mattered. That's what happens when you hold a feeling inside and keep pushing it down as deep as possible until you forget what is important to you. But after every storm comes renewal. What followed, the journey to finding "me," was the most difficult for my heart. I looked in the mirror and realized that I was a taker, shallow and selfish. Not good traits for a husband and father. That's when I decided to change. At that point, I was broken, alone, and nearly unemployable. Coming from that place rips you raw, it tears away any sense of ego, or pride until all that's left is humility.

But in that humility, you find your humanity. The giver that lives in all of us takes over.

Our mistakes are our choices that didn't quite work out, and when we have space to make mistakes because we are all holding space for each other, we are giving ourselves and everyone around us permission to try, fail and try again. And that's how we can build our dreams. It's not a straight path.

Vulnerability Lets us Love

Loving someone is scary ... loving yourself is even scarier. But both loves are critical to your growth and evolution. You don't need to be "perfect" to love or to find love. But you do need some guts. You must willingly become vulnerable, and above all else, you must become the truth.

Truth hurts. But, on the other side of hurt and pain is the love you seek. You will create a life based in truth, with an abundance of love, happiness, and possibilities.

Open your heart and be OK with taking a risk by sharing your successes and failures, your good times, and your bad times. You might hurt a little, maybe look a little foolish at times.

You will certainly figure out who you truly are and discover the path to becoming that person.

Here's the bottom line: you will never truly love another human being if you first do not love yourself. The love you give comes from your loving self. To love yourself, you must accept and embrace your truth. Be vulnerable. Create space for you to be with *you*. That's the most important thing.

I always gave away something I didn't really have. I was hurting, angry, and working through my past. Trying to love someone when I was lying to myself about who I was. I didn't even like myself. Outwardly, I was successful, but it was disingenuous, not my truth.

Accepting the truth allowed me to become the person I was born to be and opened a world of possibilities.

Finding both loves will change everything. Even if you're in a successful marriage/relationship, sit with your truth. You'll be amazed by how your love will deepen and your bond strengthens when you are vulnerable, holding space for you, for everyone you love, to be themselves in all their truth.

Being a vulnerable, unprotected soul is scary. It's like walking around naked on a cold, blustery January day. Hard to fathom, right? But, walking around with your guard up, sheathed in armor, is worse.

No matter what you do, sometimes life will hurt. You can't protect yourself from it. I was in a dark place when Doodles said that to me. He was right, nobody came to save me. It wasn't because nobody cared, I had people who loved me. But I didn't love myself. I was in pain, and ignoring it wasn't working.

I finally stumbled into a tipping point. I had only two choices left. I could be suited up in that armor of anger, safe and hidden away from life or I could be naked, vulnerable, and holding myself accountable.

What was I missing by staying in that armor? Love, forgiveness, adventure, truth. Really, everything that makes life wonderful. I had to face who I had become and tell him the truth.

Only then was he able to understand who he *could* become.

Sticktoitiveness

If you knew me between 1999 and 2009, I'm sorry. I had an angry heart and an ugly soul. I bailed on authentic living. Maybe fear got in the way. Maybe judgment and criticism wore me down. Pretty much everyone gave up on me during that time. I don't blame them; I gave up on myself. Thankfully, one person didn't give up on me. One person believed in me enough to tell me the truth.

It was me.

Final score 12/31/09: Truth 326/Jamie 0

In telling me the truth, that one person reminded me of the mercies of God and how much I've been blessed. The truth gave me the courage to be me and share the depths of my heart.

Around that time, Doodles was in my chair a lot.

Doodles was ahead of his time as an educator. He had a word he used to describe perseverance: "sticktoitiveness." I know you just chuckled reading that. It's a real word. I Googled it.

Sticktoitiveness basically means that you stick with something even when it's hard. It is one of the most important qualities we humans can develop and that makes it one of the most important things we can teach our kids.

The first step to becoming a more inspirational leader is not learning a new set of skills; it's discovering your "why," your purpose, the inspiration that sets your soul on fire. This "why" is what drives us to be more intentional in how we think, act, and live our lives. It lets us be vulnerable. Our why inspires our sticktoitiveness. And sticktoitiveness is what prevents us from ever quitting.

Like many people, when things became difficult, or uncomfortable, my default used to be, "Hey, this isn't for me, I'm out of here." Of course, that coincides with the time in my life when failure was also my default.

Again ... hello rock bottom.

Commit to putting in the work to put yourself in the best place physically, mentally, and spiritually to succeed in anything. When life places the mountain in your path, move it. Quitting is not an option. As Doodles told me several times in life: "I've yet to meet a better teacher than failure." He mentioned it during my divorce and when I was fired from a job I loved: both were my biggest failures in life, and both were my fault. I had stopped doing the work I needed to do to be successful with those. I had stopped trying.

A part of me didn't want to be vulnerable and live in my truth, so I just quit. It was easier in the short term.

Adversity enters everyone's life sooner or later. We only need to accept how blessed we are to be here. Then take personal responsibility to do something about it. Invest in you.

I know that I'm here to fill the world with my message of love and positivity. It's my calling, my mission, my holy cause ... it's my why. Show up big for everything, with a loving heart and a positive attitude. How you show up when things get rough defines you.

Don't just go through life, grow through it. Always remember: the man on top of the mountain didn't fall there, but he probably fell a few times along his own journey. When you ask him how he got there, I'm sure he will say, "With sticktoitiveness."

The morning that I made the decision to quit quitting was when I made my commitment to living each day intentionally, with unwavering purpose. The acceptance and appreciation of this beautiful gift is the first step toward an abundant life. When I put my deficiencies on display, began documenting the challenges I've faced and sharing the failures—yes, when I became vulnerable—I found the abundance that comes with living untethered.

What you see in the mirror as your flaws makes you powerful when you have the confidence to be vulnerable. The things that make you feel the most vulnerable become someone's greatest source of inspiration.

Share your story. My mission continues to be "change one life every day for the rest of my life," and I have no doubt that together we can reach the people who need to hear the message. In the process, we will change our own lives for the better.

FAITH

Life gives opportunity to each of us in its own time, in its own way. It's called "divine timing," and it's always right. Faith is having the patience to receive the opportunities as they come and follow our path.

I passed on many opportunities, or simply missed them completely because I was looking the other way. I was trying to see with my eyes what could not be seen. But faith is not visible. You can't see it or touch it. I listened when I first heard the call. But I was fearful, so I ignored it. I never mustered the courage to embrace it; rather, I grasped onto it as a lifeline when I was groping in the darkness of depression.

I didn't know it at the time, but faith is there for more than just desperation. Faith is the loving parent of Hope. Faith is not a thought. It is a feeling in your heart. When we have faith and believe in ourselves, the possibilities are limitless.

When you align with the five pillars, and sit with faith, you get your desires when the time is right. But that alignment is key. If I had been aligned to begin with, the opportunities would have been on my radar and come at just the right time, in divine timing.

Faith is a sister to Patience. Faith keeps your heart beating, your vision clear, and your spirit at peace. When you are prepared to have faith in your abilities, fear takes a back seat. Having that deep faith in your abilities is the beginning of accepting who you are.

"Faith is taking the first step even when you don't see the whole staircase." ~ Martin Luther King, Jr.

If you can see every step of your path, you're living someone else's path. Faith means taking time to be still and reflect on life's deepest questions to uncover what you truly want and then going there, even if you're going alone. Faith is love, loving every part of you, especially the messy parts. Allowing yourself to be vulnerable. Loving your shortcomings and more freely loving others.

Faith is gratitude, being grateful for all the miracles you take for granted. Faith is learning, being a student of life, never ceasing to grow. Sit in the front row of life with wonder and be in awe of its pure beauty. Faith is kind and strong, forgiving yourself, and then others, standing for something and someone. Give yourself permission to have faith, to dream big and bold without any hesitation, to feel uncomfortable.

When you reach the end of your comfort zone, lean in a little more. Faith lets you be pushed to your edge. That's the point.

Faith over Fear

Being raised Catholic, when I embarked on my own spiritual journey, the way I understand faith changed. When I think of faith now, I think of Terrilynn. Over the course of our life together, there have been milestone years: 2000, 2005, 2010, 2015, 2020, and 2023. Each represents a defining moment in our relationship. If you look at that timeline and only see 23 years, you must look closer. Look behind the numbers and you'll see love defined. You'll see a life transformed. You'll see gratitude grown from humility, patience grown from anger, wisdom grown from compassion, peace grown from chaos, and love and grace grown from faith.

In the immediate aftermath of divorce, there is pain, sometimes a lot of it. Divorce leaves an open wound that you will carry for a long time. Even if you're one of those rare souls strong enough to close that wound, the pain will linger and leave a visible scar. On top of the pain, you must go about rebuilding your life. It's hard to build a life in the best of times, let alone rebuild one from the ashes of the bonfire that was your life.

Faced with rebuilding my broken life and mending fractured relationships, I made another strategic mistake. Without even taking a breath, I tried building a new relationship. If you're thinking that was a bad idea ... you're right. There was no visible path, no roadmap to guide me, so naturally, I just made it up as I went. It proved to be a more difficult task than I could ever have imagined.

During this time, I learned about the Lighthouse vs. Tugboat parable. You see, lighthouses and tugboats serve a similar purpose, they both guide boats to safety. But they do it in entirely different ways. Tugboats go out into the ocean, and they tug huge ships back to the port. They push and pull, and they give their all to bring the boat back to safety. They work so hard to get the boat and themselves back to the port that they in turn wear themselves down.

Lighthouses shine their light to guide boats to safety. They are rooted and tall, they weather the storms, and guide the boats to port. They are always a beacon, but whether the boat driver chooses to use the light as a guide is up to the boat. It doesn't affect the lighthouse either way. The lighthouse continues to shine its light, it does not wear down in its effort.

There have been many tugboats along my journey; most came with the best of intentions. Of course, some were disguised as tugboats but only wanted to kick me when I was down. That's the thing about tugboats: you can't always tell the difference. Even the most compassionate tugboats left a mark. One collision after another, one pushing, one pulling. I was knocked around pretty good.

When I crashed straight into the rocky shore, literally no one was surprised, except me. I was becoming so well-known at rock bottom, I started receiving mail there. With the very real chance I would lose Terrilynn looming, I surrendered. I went to the place all sinners, saints, winners, and losers always end up: faith. Faith is the lighthouse that guides us in our darkest moments. A loving heart sees the beautiful truth in your mirror every morning.

Faith unlocked my loving heart and opened the door to our beautiful life together. Faith gave us the strength to live the story in our hearts. In life, if you don't like your story, you can turn the page and start writing a new chapter.

We chose to build our relationship on a strong foundation of faith. We put our faith in God and in each other. When your mind is full of chaos, you're at your most vulnerable. You don't know where to turn, and soon, the burden on your heart becomes too heavy to carry. It becomes difficult to control the debilitating negative self-talk, and that nearly ended our relationship before it started. Thankfully, Terrilynn listened to her heart, and trusted the love she carried there ... something she would have to do too often over our years together.

I have tested Terrilynn's faith more than once. She has wavered at times, but she never gave up on me. Being faithful to your heart will carry you through the most difficult times. But every heart has its limits, and faith isn't indestructible.

I have never been easy for Terrilynn. As the failures mounted and reached a crescendo in 2012, her faith was tested. My estrangement from my children grew wider, the darkness returned, and my depression grew deeper. I wasn't up to the task of holding us together. But I learned that when you join hands with someone in faith and hold on tight, your faith will always lead you to where you belong. I have always belonged wherever Terrilynn is. It was faith that reminded me of that and led me back to her. It was faith that opened her heart and welcomed me home. Love never fails when built upon a solid foundation of faith.

But faith doesn't mean a lack of fear. It means that you believe you can overcome your fears.

I am afraid. I'm afraid nearly every day because I'm determined to push my limits as far as possible. I've talked about being fearless often. But being fearless doesn't mean we are never afraid. It's *overcoming* those moments when we're afraid. It's faith over fear.

What scares me? Going backward, repeating past mistakes. Writing scares me. Fatherhood scares me. I live every day trying to fill my father's shoes, knowing full well I most likely never will.

I truly love being a father. But I fear I haven't done it well. I pray there are times my son remembers fondly. I pray there were lessons he learned as a son that he now finds valuable as a father. I pray that, in 20 years, he and I will look back and say, "Remember when …" And I pray he tells his daughters, "Your grandpa and I used to …"

We're all scared of something, sometime. But I don't avoid fear. When I say I'm "fearless," it's because I've overcome fear and won't let it determine any outcome. I've chosen faith over fear. I've chosen to believe that things will work out the way that they are supposed to. I've chosen to believe in divine timing. I've chosen to believe that the lessons I need to learn are the ones I've been presented with, and yeah, I'm finally learning them.

Our bodies only go where our minds lead, which is why choosing is so important. First, you must believe; then comes faith. Belief is thought; it's of the mind. Faith is action; it's of the body. Faith is putting your belief into action. Faith sometimes leaps, sometimes steps, and sometimes even crawls. But faith never retreats. The path will not always be clear, but you must have faith in that first step. The action that lights the path forward.

Faith is ignoring the million reasons why you wouldn't, couldn't, shouldn't—and instead listening to the one reason you should.

Faith is the companion of courage and the enemy of fear. Faith goes the extra mile.

As we move along our life's journey, our faith deepens. Our step quickens. We become bolder. Our burden becomes lighter. Even though we can see the end, we keep moving forward as though we have a million miles to go. Because we have no fear. That is faith.

Faith in our Path

The funny thing about faith is that it doesn't give us a map. It gives us heart. I believe that we can create the world that we want to live in.

A few years ago, I burned out. After spending 25 years in the engineering business, I found that I no longer wanted to put profit before people. My focus was turning away from the revenue-generating potential of projects to focusing on their human impacts. During this same time, I began exploring my life and realized what's most important to me.

I may have been a successful money-maker—but I was not a successful human being.

This transformation has helped me prioritize my days around quality, peace, and happiness. Love always reveals itself in unexpected people and places. But I needed faith in the path that I was meant to take, faith in people over profit, to make it work.

We talk to kids about getting on that track of success—you know, go to college, get a good job, and make money. I had a good job making good money. But what I didn't know, and it took me years to know, is that our hearts have a different perspective. I found my feet pointed in the right direction when I began following my heart. As I soon came to find out, empathy is the language of leadership.

Faith alone will put you on the right path, but it won't get you all the way there. For me, forward progress and growth has always followed change, as has the courage to do something different ... to *be* different. Having faith that something greater was at work made those times of change easier, but I discovered that I had to hold up my end of the deal. My part was to do the right things for myself and for others, to live with integrity, and stop lying. Those are our own individual responsibilities.

When you accept those responsibilities, you will understand and believe that there is something greater watching over you, reminding you to be a good person and not just show up, but show up powerfully and have faith in your path.

Faith in Yourself

Everything I have in my life is because of the faith I have in myself. I have shown up every day and done the work. Everything in life starts with one step: a step into faith. It's faith that allows us to believe in our ability to create, build, and succeed. Faith fuels our purpose.

Faith is found in trust. I found the path to having faith in myself by letting go of everything I thought I knew. That is difficult for most people, and I'm no different. My father always preached, "control the controllables." It showed up first in my professional life. I knew I would never be the smartest person in the room ... but I could be the hardest worker.

You must, above all else, believe in yourself. If you don't, you cannot expect anyone else to believe in you. Life has an interesting way of testing our resolve. Either by having nothing happen at all or having everything happen at once. Yes, having too many opportunities is the same as having no opportunities.

You must be in alignment—mind, body, and spirit—with your purpose, have faith in yourself, to stay on your path, choose the right opportunities, and meet your goals in divine timing.

Otherwise, you'll become overwhelmed when opportunity comes knocking.

Have faith in yourself and in something bigger than you. Regardless of what you do for a living, live so your life is changing the lives of others and impacting generations. Appreciate the moments that breathe purpose and love into your life. Be confident in the choices you make. Share the passions of your heart, and the creativity of your thoughts.

Be brave enough to do these things, and when the call comes, you will answer it.

Faith over Failure

I've experienced so many things in my life, good and bad, that continue to mold me into the man that I believe God has planned for me to become. I've been diverted to a path that I haven't navigated before. But I believe I'm where I'm supposed to be at this point in my life. We can lose everything we have ever known, or everyone we have ever loved. I've been there. I've failed publicly, been financially broken, and lost people who I love more than words. In those times we must learn, grit our teeth through the pain, and push forward on the slow walk toward a better life.

It's been some time now since I stopped hiding from my failures. For a long time, I struggled to get past every stumble. I never learned how to deal with the little setbacks and challenges. When faced with real adversity—divorce—I responded as badly as possible. I did everything wrong. Simply put, I was an ass.

To this day, many years later, it still haunts me.

I can tell you from that experience, failure doesn't define you if you don't let it. Make no mistake: life takes balance, pulling from both directions. You must experience the dark to embrace the light. Your heart knows the way to the light.

Because my faith is stronger than my failure, I now speak my truth. I still stumble now and then, but we're all a work in progress. Life is painting a masterpiece you will never see completed. Have faith and make bold strokes.

The ego resides in fear of failure. The heart resides in faith.

Faith and God

I was raised in the Catholic Church in the Mon Valley by people who worked hard and helped each other, pretty much unconditionally. We were in this life together ... an entire community of different people, all God's beautiful creation living and working together. In the time of my youth, it was almost the perfect life ...

Then something changed: I grew up.

As a young adult, I had a tenuous relationship with God. I didn't realize that I was trying to fit Him into a mold of what I wanted Him to be. As a result, my faith was shaken to its very core. I walked away. I started looking for meaning.

Then, in the wake of a succession of traumatic experiences, I surrendered. I let go of those false expectations. Then I allowed Him to mold me into the person He made me to be.

After much searching and experiences, good and bad, I don't consider myself a religious man. I am, however, very spiritual, and my faith in God is strong. My faith fuels my purpose. My faith is what drives me to always do the right thing.

God does not give us the opportunity to discover the perfect life for ourselves. Nobody can successfully navigate this journey we call life alone. That's why God does give us the opportunity to build the perfect life for each other.

I have faith that every experience will make me a better man. It hasn't always been that way. I haven't always had faith in God's calling in my life. But I realized that I needed to find my path, and to find my path, I needed my faith. If you're searching for your path, create space to be quiet with yourself and listen carefully, your intuition will always lead you to your purpose.

"Let me tell you what God knows ..."

My dad always led with that when he was about to drop some raw truth on someone. We always knew something impactful was coming, something from his heart, and we'd best be paying attention.

One of the big truths he shared with me was that failure only defeats you if you allow it. Faith buoys you through failure. God created your path. You just need to walk in faith.

Faith guides us through change, but change is still scary. Change doesn't happen overnight. It requires stick-to-it-iveness, perseverance, determination, and grit. But the most undeniably critical component of success is faith.

The most dynamic and successful leaders are confident in who they are and have become the best they can be by depending on God, on their faith, for help.

Believe

That's one of my favorite words. Believe. One powerful, life-changing word. Life will challenge you. It will be messy, even ugly at times. You can't just wish it pretty.

You will become stronger or weaker in adversity. It depends solely on your reaction. You must believe in you. Have faith because you can run, but you can't hide from who you are. You are you, and who you will become is determined by who you believe you are right now.

Nobody is immune to life's challenges. But at any given moment, you have the power to change your life. All you need to do is believe. You must always remember that. Your past doesn't define you. Circumstances don't define you. The choices you make will define you and determine the path your life will follow.

Those challenges? Love them. Look for them. Embrace them. Attack them voraciously. In fact, don't get comfortable waiting for life to challenge you. Get uncomfortable by challenging yourself. Become stronger, smarter ... and happier.

Never let a single day pass by without doing something you can be proud of. Life is never about what happens to you; it's always about how you respond to it.

Sometimes the path that God has for your life looks drastically different than you may have dreamed. Keep believing in the path.

At the beginning of your journey, your story is merely a blank page that represents potential. If you're like me ... you stepped into the unknown and were willing to embrace whatever came your way. Then, as you navigated the twists and turns, ups and downs of life ... the depth and breadth of your experience became fuller.

Before you knew it, the page no longer represented your potential, but rather, became your story of the hard work, pain and sadness, grit and determination, joy and fulfillment ... and the strong mindset that brought you here. This journey we're sharing can be grueling; it's repetitive and boring, yet at times thrilling and chaotic. After a while, I started to think … "What am I doing here? I didn't sign up for this."

That moment is when I understood the reason why you and I were brave enough to take on this journey in the first place. We're adventurous souls who want to uncover what we're made of. I've learned that my body can keep pushing long after my mind has screamed for it to stop, and my mind can pull my body through adversity long after it has surrendered.

I may not be on the journey of my choosing, but it's the perfect one for me. Expand your comfort zone … become the person God calls you to be and tell your story.

There is a plan for each of us. We have a path to walk, and when we stray too far off course, God taps us on the shoulder: "OK, Jamie time to course correct and re-center. You have a lot more to do here."

Tap …

Everything happens for a reason. No matter where you are, or what adversity is placed in your path … take care not to stray too far, lest you lose yourself. Believe and never lose hope. Hope may not change the circumstance, it may not change the outcome … but when we believe, it changes us. And that is enough.

Tap …

It wasn't fate or destiny, or anything else that brought me to this place in life. It was the plan. It doesn't matter what's been written in your story so far, it's how you fill up the rest of the pages that counts.

The Person in the Chair

God's not done with you yet.

ACCEPTANCE

Faith overcomes your fear of vulnerability. Self-acceptance follows closely behind your faith. The act of accepting who and where you are right now, and being present in that space, guides you away from insecurity.

When the noise from outside seeps within, you become distracted from your heart, and bogged down in the mud. Even the lightest weight you may carry becomes a heavy burden. Being present in your life and accepting yourself, accepting your flaws and imperfections, will quiet the outside noise so your inner voice may be clearly heard.

When I was in the dark, wallowing in self-pity, being vulnerable terrified me. After all, I was a man, a warrior, a provider. At least, I was told that I should be afraid of being vulnerable, but that kept me hiding on rock bottom for far too long. The darkness of depression is powerful and mysterious. Even when one knows that place as intimately as I do, it is hard to understand, and even harder to explain.

You can do everything right, and someone will still react negatively and criticize you. That negativity grows from the seeds of anger, jealousy, and disrespect planted by others. Understanding that nobody needs to accept you other than you deflects any negativity thrown your way and puts control of your life firmly in your hands.

Who are You?

There's no way to avoid the question, "Who am I?" Sometimes, it's challenging or uncomfortable to answer it. While it's true that life doesn't have an easy button, it does have a reset button. Accepting who we are allows us to accept what we have chosen, or at least our role in how our lives play out, which in turn, lets us find that reset, allowing us to build upon our rock bottom.

Losing a job, a marriage, literally a family, forces you to reassess your choices and value system. It forces you to look inward and ultimately provides the courage to lean into adversity. It also presents an opportunity for a reinvention of yourself.

I was a great father to my children. I did everything right. Unfortunately, I was a lousy husband to their mother. I did everything wrong. I could tell you that I was too young, but that would just be an excuse. I knew what I was doing. I could tell you that it was her fault ... that she didn't love me enough. Blah, blah, blah ... more excuses.

The truth is, I didn't *let* her love me because I didn't love myself. I didn't know how to be loved. Our divorce, the most negative experience of my life, was my fault. All of it. I tried to hide from it, but it found me. I tried to run from it, but of course it caught me.

Robert Frost wrote, "The only way out is through." This is absolutely true. Of course, you can hide, you can run, you can blame others. But when you exhaust those options, "through" is the only choice. The road to redemption goes straight through that obstacle. Along that road, you're going to encounter all the demons from your past. I had to face mine, and there were many. And they piled on.

Demons are like that. They'll stay with you and kick you when you're down. The demons that led to divorce and estrangement from my children followed me to Terrilynn. Her strength proved to be too much for them. Her strength carried us both through the hardest times.

I believe redemption is a long road that has no end; you walk it for the rest of your life. Still a little wobbly from repeated body blows resulting from divorce, it took me some time, a few years in fact, to find my footing. Self-inflicted or not, it was real. I was blessed to have someone to steady my steps and pick me up when I was reduced to a crawl. I've encountered many others on this road, and I will always be the first to extend a hand. Nobody needs to take this journey alone.

If you're reading this and feel lost, look closely at the road ahead. I've left footprints for you to follow.

When life gave me a chance at redemption, I grabbed it with both hands. I'm still challenged daily and forced to make choices. But those choices that once came from desperation now come from inspiration. Every challenge I have faced in my life has been an opportunity for transformation. The circumstances I've encountered along my journey have been both bad and good. I'm not the product of those circumstances. I'm entirely the product of my choices. Those rooted in desperation defined who I was and those lifted by inspiration define who I have become.

The most important relationship you will ever build is with you. Because your purpose is you. That's where everything begins. Your holy cause grows from within. Find the courage to be authentic and be at peace with your imperfections. Accept them. Be honest about your weaknesses and learn to be strong. Admit how much you don't know and learn what you need.

Don't try to be perfect, try to be authentic, and learn to be yourself. Have the courage to fail and learn to succeed.

Failure is still the world's greatest teacher. Failure, no matter how many times you do it, doesn't diminish your human value. You will not add value to others if you don't first believe in your self-worth. Gratitude comes from the courage to learn to love who you are and your place in the world.

Accept the past. Regrets, I've had a few. Everyone knows regret. We all have something we regret saying, doing, or not doing. Most people fear failure. They fear what others will think of them. I've learned to love and accept failure. My only fear is regret. I dragged the chains of regret around for a long time, so I know how damaging they can be. It took a long time to break the chains of regret. My fear is that I may pick them up again.

Sometimes, I'll be walking forward, and glance left or right and see those old rusty chains. But I remember that this is my story and no one else's. So, I leave them where they are. I'll take all the discomfort in the world to avoid regret. My decisions are part of me, and I accept them.

You Choose

I often think about my own journey through life, and I'm proof that eventually, you must let go of who you once were to discover who you truly are and what you're truly capable of. At some point in time, you're going to find your true self, find what's important to you. I had to stand on rock bottom and search within myself for a connection with something greater than me. That connection drives me to become more because I chose to focus on it. I accepted who I was and who I could be and actively chose to pursue my path.

Choose to focus on who you are, not what you're not. Much like you, I'm a mix of unlikely things you would not guess by looking at me. I'm comfortable in the skin I'm in. Perhaps balding, middle-aged guys with glasses aren't your cup of tea, so you'll pass on my story. But what might you be missing?

Choose to accept all people for who they are, not what they look like. Choose to respect others and give them the same opportunity to tell their story. Everything that happens on that journey is divinely placed just for you, so you find your true self and fulfill your life purpose. It will be challenging, and the choice to accept the challenge is up to you. This journey is meant to be an adventure, so choose to take chances, connect the dots, and collect experiences. You just might learn something.

Accepting your path might be scary, but you always have the power to change your life. You always have a choice. The easy path is never rewarding.

There are five steps to becoming the best version of you and succeeding at anything you choose:

Step 1: State your goal (write it down/tell people).

Step 2: Believe you can achieve it.

Step 3: Focus on your goal.

Step 4: Take action.

Step 5: Repeat (as many times as necessary).

You will fail. You will want to quit. Don't ever give up on yourself. Because growth is inherently uncomfortable. It means facing who you believe you are so you can believe in who you can become. That's a difficult task.

Don't be afraid to question who you are. Only in that place can you let go of who you've been, and step into who you're becoming. I can tell you from experience, it's not for the faint of heart. I didn't like who I was for a long time.

But the only way to transform your life is through daily practice. You can.

In a world where you can be anything you want, what would you choose to be? It's not what you want that makes you powerful, it's what you're willing to be and the work you're willing to do. Choose to be. Accept the power of being.

BE the leader you wish you had. BE the friend you wish you had. BE the spouse you desire.

You receive what you give. BE that which you want in your life.

Yes, accept the past. Accept who you were. But drive to be more.

What impact do you want to have on the world? Fate will send us messages if we're paying attention. But that doesn't mean we must blindly obey and accept. We always have a choice. Some of those choices can be game-changers.

I choose to do these four things every day:

- Never leave an "I love you" unsaid.
- Never leave a kind act undone.
- Always teach others what you know.

- Always do more than what is expected.

You can change the course of your life. All you need to do to begin creating the life you want is get out of your own way. There are no limits. There are no restrictions. You can course correct daily if necessary. The obstacles that you feel are holding you back are not outside of you; they're inside you. That stuff outside? Those are opportunities.

Choose Wisely

What an amazing time to be alive. You have choices. It's a beautiful thing. No matter what your past has thrown at you, you have the power to change your future by what you choose to do in the present. You have choices. Start today by stopping your successes from going to your head. Live in your heart, and don't let the opinion of others steal your attention. You are who you are today because of the choices you made yesterday.

You've had adversity in your life. You've been challenged, you've tried and failed. You've stumbled over one obstacle after another. Congratulations. Did you choose to quit, or did you choose to learn? If you're holding onto anger because someone did you wrong, that's your fault. If you're frustrated because you didn't reach your goals, that's on you.

I've taken the path that was meant for me. My journey is one I had to experience to become this man today. Everything that has happened to me has happened for a reason.

"If you live each day as if it were your last, someday you will most certainly be right."

Diamonds. Gold. Today.

Every today is precious. Sooner or later, we all will run out of tomorrows. Remember yesterday, prepare for tomorrow. Just don't let them take too much of today. We have one common destination that none of us can escape.

Give each today of your life the respect it deserves.

Life has punched me in the gut more than once. One of those punches left me on my knees. I was at the end, there was no way I was standing back up, not from this one. Since I was already on my knees ... I prayed. It was perhaps the first legitimate prayer of my life. I cried ... I prayed hard at that moment. Then I stood up.

I have never wasted a moment of life since.

You have an expiration date. Until then, go big. Live passionately, love deeply and freely. Don't hold anything back. You have nothing to lose, so choose. There is no embarrassment, no failure to fear. There is only living YOUR life, on YOUR terms. Be intentional, live each precious day on purpose. Even if you spend today doing nothing, recharging, resting, there is purpose in that.

Choose today. Choose happy. Today, we will have challenges sent our way, I'm sure. Accept them and grow. And I'm just as sure we will have beautiful gifts presented to us as well. We must be open to both. Today the world won't be perfect, but you can choose to make it perfect for you. There is no right or wrong today. You can't make a bad choice. Today is there for YOU to choose happy or sad, brave or afraid, succeed or fail. Nobody defines YOUR today but YOU.

If this was your last today, what would you do? Whatever you do today, make it yours. Live it ... really live it. Live your perfect today … whatever that is in your heart. Don't settle, and lead with love.

Leading with love is about seeing the world as it truly is, through the lens of curiosity, courage, wisdom, and truth. It's about acceptance. Choose to lead with love in everything you do. Choose to be kind to everyone you meet. Choose to help others walk with hope. Choose to impact lives positively.

"Instead of thinking how hard your journey is, think of how great your story will be." ~ Andy Frisella

Memories fade, but they never truly leave us. In fact, some memories linger for a lifetime. I used to think that I could forget the bad memories if I just put them out of my mind … until I started writing. However, we're not the things that happened to us.

I'm grateful for each and every life experience that I have been given. All of them have made a difference. Each and every one has been a blessing and has made me the man I am today.

Life is a beautiful masterpiece bound together by your experiences. You were created with a purpose; you matter. Your life, your heart and soul, your hopes and dreams … it all matters. I am proof that broken things can be made whole once more.

I no longer hide from bad memories. Now I know they are priceless because I choose to let them remind me of how far I've come. There have been many times when, standing on the edge of giving up, I took one more step forward instead. I chose to be the person I want to be and accepted who I am.

Self-acceptance is found wrapped in your faith. It is the harvest you reap after sowing the seeds of vulnerability, and the key that unlocks the door to accountability.

ACCOUNTABILITY

Everything bad that has happened in your life that stemmed from your actions and choices is your fault.

This statement might land pretty hard, but it's the truth.

Accountability is more than accepting responsibility for your words and actions. It is acknowledging that you have had a hand in defining everything that has happened in your life, good and bad. You had to choose how you were impacted by each experience. Joy and sadness are choices. Gratitude is a choice (we'll talk about that in the next chapter).

In response to the actions of another, you get to choose to love them or hate them. Accountability is fully owning everything that happens in your life.

Becoming accountable for my words and actions illuminated the lessons I missed and brought a calm understanding to every experience. Accountability made me grateful for the opportunity to become a better man and put my feet on the path to the highest version of myself.

Accountability is ownership, the opposite of blame. It's easy and comfortable to blame others. It covers our weaknesses and shortcomings. Our first thought when we fail is often to excuse it away by blaming someone or something. Being accountable is accepting and acknowledging the failure, learning from it, and growing that lesson into success.

For the first 40 years of my life, I never made a mistake, never lost at anything. There was always someone to blame or something unforeseen that was the culprit for any negative outcome. For example, everyone was responsible for my divorce except the one person most responsible. Of course, that would be me.

Accountability will reveal gifts that you had previously hidden from yourself. Becoming accountable will provide clarity and lift the cloud of negativity that surrounds the denial of responsibility.

The day I finally held myself accountable was the darkest of my life. There was anger from the pain I felt and regret from the pain I caused. There was emptiness caused by the sadness of a life unlived. Cynics will say I was backed into a corner and had no other choice. That's understandable to the casual critic, I mean "observer." The truth is, I had two people, one on each side of me, personal and professional, who pulled me to the path I have walked ever since.

Through my 20s and 30s, I didn't know why I was here, or what the point of it all could possibly be. I didn't have a purpose, and therefore, I had no real sense of myself. I wandered along my journey through life with no real path forward, doing just enough to get by. I saw someone who appeared to be successful, and I started down their path ... then another, and another, trying to make one my own. But none really fit because they weren't meant for me. All I was doing was walking in circles.

You won't find the path meant for you if you hide from your heart.

In my confusion, I accepted what others were telling me, and I slowly started hating myself.

Welcome Bruce Fletcher to the jungle. I met Bruce on the day I interviewed for a project manager position. This was, at the time, an opportunity I didn't think was possible—the one that would take me from a job that paid the bills to a career that would lead me to the top of my profession. From that first handshake, I knew this cat was different. Much like Terrilynn, I still can't tell you what Bruce saw in me, but he is as responsible for who I've become as anyone in my life. Bruce taught me business and gave me responsibility. He held me accountable beyond my project responsibilities. He held me accountable for my words and actions in the office. Bruce is a brilliant strategist, and he wisely kept me on a short leash, at first.

Despite Bruce's and Terrilynn's best efforts, I struggled to find balance in my personal and professional life. When things were good with Terrilynn, I stumbled at work. When things were falling into place at the office, it seemed things were falling apart at home. Bruce finally sat me down and told me something profound. He said, "You can't get away from yourself. It doesn't matter what you do, how often you try to hide, or how far you run. You are always with you." I remember Doodles telling me that there are only three things that we control in our lives: what we think, what we look at, and the actions we take.

Just like that, it started making sense.

Most of my adult years were spent groping around in the dark. I lived the first 45 years of my life without intention. Bouncing from one random experience to another is how we lose ourselves. And I was lost at sea, drifting aimlessly on a current not of my choosing. I learned the hard way that to receive what you want from life you must first give it away. Only then was I able to swim to the life preserver that Terrilynn had thrown into the water to save me.

Be kind, and random acts of kindness will follow you wherever you go. If you want respect, you must respect others. If you want to fall in love, love yourself first. That's how accountability works.

Accountability Runs Deep

Accountability is hard. It's a vulnerable process, and we humans are averse to vulnerability. We think we must always be strong. The truth is that allowing ourselves to be vulnerable takes more strength than most can muster. Most of all, it exposes our weaknesses to ourselves.

In my journey with depression, I had to learn accountability in a good way (ownership rather than blaming myself) and how to handle the feelings that come with it. Everyone has been depressed, lonely, or unhappy at some time in their life. Perhaps right now. We often pretend we don't have feelings. That we don't hurt. That we don't feel alone or depressed. There's no feeling in life more suffocating than feeling alone. Nothing can prepare you for the amount of darkness that feeling brings.

Depression looks just like me. Loneliness looks just like you. Unhappiness lives right down the street. Winning doesn't help. Success is not a cure. Those feelings are there regardless, and often, accountability is the trigger. We realize we are to blame, and sometimes, we take more credit than we deserve for what happened. It can bring us to our knees.

We need to approach accountability from an empowered stance. Yes, I did this. This is what I learned. Now, I can do better. Because I failed at marriage, I'm a better husband. Because I failed as a father, I'm a better grandfather. It sounds simple, and it can be. But always remember to get some help if that darkness is too dark for too long. We may be lonely, but we don't need to do this journey alone.

What I've learned about accountability from Doodles and then my friend Bruce as they sat in my chair is that life may not always be easy, but it is always simple. You show up and do what's required. Yes, sometimes to do what is required takes a Herculean effort. But remember this: nobody is making the wheel rounder or the water more wet.

Surround yourself with good people and learn from them. Always grow from what you learn, especially as you're holding yourself accountable for the not-so-great stuff.

Don't sugar-coat your story so it's easier to swallow. The truth you haven't told yourself is the freedom you've yet to gain. Accountability is the first step to success. And accountability starts with being honest with yourself. It changed my life immensely. Looking in the mirror with honesty and accountability was like getting punched in the face. It hurt, because all the crap in my life, the mistakes, the failures, the hurt ... all the things that caused me to sink into depression ... all of it was my fault.

Have you ever looked in the mirror and told yourself the truth? That's when my life changed. One day while shaving, I stopped what I was doing and literally looked in the mirror. I don't know why I stopped, but I stared for a minute and said, "You let you down."

I said it out loud. That's the moment I took ownership of all of it. And I've owned it ever since. This wasn't an "aha" moment where the fog lifted and I suddenly could see. It was nothing that dramatic. It was a simple moment of telling myself the truth. I didn't reach that moment alone. I was dragging that stuff around for years, keeping it buried deep inside, and deflecting it in the form of blame on everyone else.

That stuff is heavy. It's a burden few can bear. That stuff is ACCOUNTABILITY. Perhaps the most feared word in the English language.

Your past cannot define you. You either focus on the past, the failures, the things that didn't work and things out of your control, or you focus on what you *can* control, the required action, and all the possibilities in front of you.

Accountability is Truth

Accountability is key for you to grow and thrive as a human being. Growth ... that constant human state of becoming, is interrupted when accountability is absent. You become stagnant, and you regress.

When I finally told myself the truth, it hurt. It was my fault. I was waking up accidentally every morning and living nowhere near my ability. I wasn't living my purpose. I wasn't living *on* purpose. I was ignoring the people in the chair, and I certainly didn't have my five pillars lined up.

I needed a hard reality check. That's when I realized I wasn't being real with myself till that moment. I have learned so much about myself during my journey to accountability. My heart is full every day I get to open my eyes. I am grateful. I have a positive mindset. I'm an unrealistic dreamer, and I create my reality. My perception of the world around me is positive. I know it's real because I'm creating it.

I read about the importance of routine and building non-negotiables into our days. Morning coffee, meditation, and yoga are three things I've come to depend on. Three things that have developed my mind, opened my heart, and deepened my faith. These are the things that keep me real. These are the core of my morning routine. I think; then I write. These are my non-negotiables. They help me be accountable because I'm actively implementing them in my life, starting my day with intention, claiming my life as my own. They are building me into the person I am to become.

Embracing the day is so much better than facing the day.

Accountability starts with being honest with yourself. You'll never be accountable for your past or responsible for your future if you can't be honest with yourself in the present.

Own your story. Life is not easy. If you're one of the crazy ones like me who believe you can make an impact on this world, then you know that won't come without sacrifice.

Perhaps the greatest light in life comes from those willing to endure the most darkness.

Blame Game

What do you do when God gives you a plan for your life, but the plan never happens?

I learned my most important lesson about success after getting fired from the best job I ever had. After working for 15 years for a local engineering firm, I was hired by a national firm. I believed this offered me everything I wanted: big projects, travel to major cities around the country, a great salary. God laid out a plan for me and everything was falling into place. The problem? Me. I wasn't ready. So, I burned it all to the ground, all of it— my job, my marriage ... my life.

Even my dog left me. God's plan was no longer recognizable.

Of course, in that moment I blamed everyone, even the dog, poor guy. The finger-pointing only led to more bad choices. But someone had to be responsible for my mess. Guess whose fault it was? Sometimes you get the thing you thought you wanted ... but it doesn't give you what you *need*. It turns out that this was part of God's plan for me.

There was something much bigger in play than losing a job.

I was fighting and losing a lifelong battle with depression ... and didn't even know it. Part of the problem was that I didn't own that I had control of my life.

Today, I have no excuses. No blame. I own it. My choices. My journey. My life. I've taken a circuitous route to becoming *me*. And I now know that no journey worth taking is a straight line. Own your mistakes, but don't ever let them own you. The extent to which you can achieve your dreams depends on the extent to which you take responsibility for your life.

Responsibility is a choice. No spin, no lies, no hiding. I have written about the missing pieces of my heart. Well, those pieces are missing because of choices I made. Poor choices, to say the least. Our choices generate a powerful ripple effect that not only impacts our lives, but the lives of those around us as well. Choosing to accept responsibility for our actions is one of the most courageous human acts.

Living well is a choice. Your life is the greatest masterpiece you can ever create. Your choices will determine who you are and who you will become. Take great care in choosing. One choice can change everything. The difference between who you are now and who you were five years ago is largely due to how well you've learned the lessons along the way.

Today is a new day that has been handed to you. You have a choice—so get out there and create a masterpiece!

If you could open a door and go anywhere, where would you go? Would you go back in time and reinvent yourself? Tempting, I'll admit. But I would not go backward. I would stay the course, mistakes and all. And there have been many. They made me who I am because I've learned from them. I've gotten to a place where I realize that I have a good life and the only way to get there is to keep looking forward, putting in the work, and never surrendering.

I'm not that good at anything in particular; I just knew I was capable of more, so I jumped in the deep end and refused to sink.

You have an impact in every situation, whether intentional or not. You must be bold, you must go for it, and you must embrace the mistakes that you make along the way. You're doing yourself, your community, and your family a disservice if you play it safe. It's easy to go through life just accepting things for the way they are.

Seek out criticism. It makes us better. Embrace adversity. It makes us stronger. Do things that scare us. It makes us fearless. So, don't be afraid to just start. Just do it.

It's how we change the story from things that happen to us to things that happen *because* of us.

Choose Your Path

Like it or not, you are the trail you've left behind. The past doesn't define your life, but it's part of you. There's no sense hiding from that trail. You can't just drop it by the side of the road and walk away. There will always be that trail of breadcrumbs to lead you back to it. You can choose to follow those breadcrumbs back ...

OR

You can choose to stop dragging the past around. You can choose to stop using the past as an excuse. You can choose ownership of, and accountability for, the past. You can learn from the past. You can overcome the past. For me, I know who I am. Because I learned and grew into me. I'm comfortable in this skin, but it wasn't always so. Your worth as a human being is non-negotiable. It's not found in anyone else—it's only found in your own heart.

Sharing the pain of your journey is powerful. To fully own and share it takes guts. The people you will influence will learn, grow, and become from your pain. When you spend your life exploring, learning, giving, teaching, working, and becoming ... you undoubtedly have experienced pain. AND you've left a trail.

Own it, because what comes next is the real you. Chose to leave those breadcrumbs to the birds.

Think about where you were five years ago. Think about how quickly those five years have passed. Think about your dream life then, your dream job, dream house. Now, ask yourself a question, "Am I closer today to who/what/where I want to be, than five years ago?" Sometimes it's easy to lose sight of where you're headed, because of where you've been.

Life has a way of, well, getting in the way. Don't ask that question in five years and find yourself still right here. Say "yes." Get out there. And if it scares you, that's awesome, and even more reason to say "yes" and get after it. Commit fully to your dream and focus your energy on that path.

I fell short as a husband and father for years. The guilt and regret paralyzed me. It made me angry and fearful; it kept me frozen in time. I couldn't get past that place. I thought things happened *to* me, never *because of* me.

Life will certainly bludgeon you into submission ... if you allow it. My life changed when I chose accountability over blame. I discovered that things happen because of me and not to me.

"You are the master of your fate, and the captain of your soul."
~ William Ernest Henley[3]

---

[3] Henley, W.E. "Invictus."

https://www.poetryfoundation.org/poems/51642/invictus

GRATITUDE

Accountability is the loving parent of Gratitude. Once you start owning your role in everything that happens in your life, you can move to being grateful for the lessons pulled from the challenges and adversity you encounter. Gratitude turns every challenge and adversity into a learning experience and brings them into your heart. The space that is created by gratitude pushes the negativity out and makes room for discovery of your true self.

Being thankful in times of abundance is not practicing gratitude. Being thankful for your blessings every day, especially through seasons of scarcity, helps you navigate the unpredictable seas of want and need. Gratitude for everything you have and for who you are grows when you forgive yourself.

First Comes Forgiveness

I carried the guilt of divorce forward like an anchor for years. I disguised it as anger and directed it at my ex-wife and children … as if my failure were their fault. Then I selfishly shared it with Terrilynn and her children, jeopardizing the very relationship that saved my life. It wasn't until she held me accountable for my actions that I realized the true magnitude of the pain I caused. When she didn't forgive me "fast enough," I became angrier and crashed deeper into depression.

Imagine being angry at your family for not forgiving you for something you caused in the first place.

My breakthrough in my struggle with depression came when I nearly lost Terrilynn. I sat on a bench crying—just a random bench in the pouring rain—and came face to face with the prospect of life without her.

That day, in that moment of clarity, everything changed. That day, I stopped seeking forgiveness and accepted responsibility for my actions. I started making small, daily decisions to pursue a life of purpose, and sure enough, I found the forgiveness I had been denied in an unlikely place. It was waiting in my own heart the whole time, just waiting for me to see it.

When you've been that broken, you never really become whole again. Part of me is still broken and may always be. The broken pieces I've carried with me for so long have gotten lighter. But I believe in my heart that I wouldn't be showing up today as I am if I hadn't been broken yesterday. Learning to accept and embrace my flaws and imperfections has made my life better in a million ways. Every day, a little more of our life is gone. We have fewer days left, there is just not enough time to drag every failure, every heartbreak, every "should have" and "would have," along with us on this journey.

Those things break people.

I think all of us are broken in some way ... if you've experienced life at all, you have some missing pieces. But here's the thing about broken people: they have walked through the fire well and healed their wounds.

Broken people are all around us. They will always be more truthful than most. Broken people will always be more grateful than most. Broken people will always smile bigger. They don't count their blessings, because one who has healed has known scarcity and sees abundance everywhere.

Broken people will always be more compassionate than most. They don't criticize or judge ... because one who has healed understands what giving everything you have and failing feels like. Broken people will always love deeper than most. They fall hard and fast ... because one who has healed has a heart that has been ripped to shreds and spent a lifetime stitching it back together.

Broken people pray harder than most. Their souls shine brightly ... because one who has healed has lost hope in the darkness and shares the light in faith.

I wouldn't change a thing about where I've been. Looking over my shoulder from this place, I realize that everything had to happen the way it did to make me into the person I am now. I walk in my truth every day as the best version of me. I never respected the man I was, let alone loved him, until I became the person I am. When you love who you are and honor your journey, you will learn to love the experiences that shaped you and learn from them.

I learned to forgive myself so I could be grateful for who I was and what I had. Life, for the first time, meant something. It was a tough process. The path to gratitude goes through acceptance, forgiveness, and accountability.

Grateful is Hopeful

You are given two choices in life: you can accept things as they are or take responsibility for changing them. There are moments in life that define you ... and they don't happen on the victory podium. They don't happen when you receive that promotion. They don't happen when the struggle ends. The moments that define you build your strength. They're the clay that molds your character. They give you depth and substance. They break your heart to show you love.

They are the moments dripping with your blood, sweat, and tears that give you the smile the world sees.

Be grateful for them. Appreciating the past gives us hope for tomorrow.

People will relate more to your real life than the "perfect" life that you think they want to see. That's average, it's mediocre, not to mention a little cowardly. You're a masterpiece in progress, and some of your most beautiful moments happen long before your victory lap. I'm grateful for my every failure.

I'm grateful for my broken heart. I'm grateful for my depression. I'm grateful for my imperfections.

I'm grateful for my bumps, bruises, and scars.

Why am I grateful for these unfortunate things? Because of them, I learned how to succeed, how to love, how to have a positive impact, how to be my best—and most importantly, how to have the courage to change. Don't settle for only showing the world your finished product. You're deeper and more complex than that. Those moments when you may be sad, disheartened, disheveled, embarrassed, or just a bit out of sync are the most important moments in your life ... too important to hide. Be grateful for them.

I woke up one day, partway through my gratefulness journey, to a strange feeling, it wasn't my usual morning. The gratitude was there, but something was off. Something was missing. This went on for five or six days, becoming increasingly scattered. Then I got it; it just hit me: I let someone inside my head. Their negativity had weaved its way into my mindset. This happened because I had become too comfortable and settled ... and was hiding from my truth. I had forgotten what it felt like to be excited about the future, the future that I was hopeful for because I was grateful for the lessons that were taking me there. I had forgotten why I started ... that feeling I had, when I committed to the future, the freedom ... the feeling that the weight of the world had been lifted off my shoulders.

You can't hide behind the stories you tell yourself. Your truth will always find you. It always knows where you're hiding. Real stories, like our real lives, don't always have happy endings. Even life's happy endings are full of sacrifice, failure, sadness, and pain.

One thing I've found in life is no matter how much you plan, bad things happen. We get divorced. We go through bankruptcies. We lose our jobs. We lose loved ones. Each one of these things can be devastating; all of them have happened to me. We all must make choices in those moments. We can choose to give in to the darkness, or we can choose to use it to motivate us forward. I chose to use them as motivation to become the best version of me possible. To be grateful for the lessons so I can be hopeful for the future.

Give and Receive

Life is giving and receiving. Gratitude, which enables us to do both, is how we assess our inner truth. When we give everything to life and are grateful for what we have, life will return these things to us in kind.

Clear your mind. Just slow down, close your eyes, and think for a moment. Focus on what is truly important in your life. Think about the things that matter.

Now ... breathe in your blessings. Breathe out your gratitude. Giving and receiving is as simple as that. Allow it. Honest gratitude for what you have is one of the building blocks for success in every aspect of your life. You may not have everything you want in your life, but you likely have everything you need. We often find ourselves frustrated because we confuse want and need. Want gives us stress. Need gives us peace.

Don't let the constant pursuit of what you want keep you from appreciating and being grateful for what you already have. When you live with purpose, you don't work for money. You work to make a difference ... and the money finds you.

Living with purpose and doing what you're called to do builds the greatest wealth you will ever know: your overall wellness.

Your wealth as a human is not measured in currency. It's your mental, physical, and spiritual health. A positive mindset, physical fitness, and being right with God will serve you far better than a few more dollars in your bank account. Let's be clear: it's perfectly ok to want more out of life. And you must put in the work to achieve anything worth having. I'm suggesting it shouldn't be your focus. By helping others find what they need, what you want will come back to you as the result of what you give.

Focusing on what you want is focusing on lack. It just increases the distance between your desire and the outcome. However, focusing on what you have and being grateful for it will bring you everything you will ever need. When you believe that you have everything you need, you open the door and invite in everything you want. Scarcity is nothing more than refusing to accept the abundance in your hands.

What you send out into the world will return to you.

I am so Grateful

This morning I'm grateful. Every morning, I'm grateful. Even if I get physically or mentally beat up, I'm always grateful for another day. I no longer feel sorry for myself because that's impossible when you're focused on helping others. No anger. No frustration. Just gratitude for the chance to learn, grow, and add value.

I have learned that when you commit to being yourself, the negativity and fear of others cannot influence your personal journey.

My morning routine always includes a little prayer of gratitude, because I know I'm blessed. I always thank God for waking me to another beautiful day. For another beautiful sunrise, and the opportunity to share it with those I love and respect. For blessing us with health and happiness. My heart is full and my will is strong because I'm so grateful for these things in my life.

If the only good thing that happens to you today is that you woke up, drop to your knees tonight, and thank God for another day. If you are able to read this book, you probably have something to be grateful for. Wake up every morning with gratitude because you've got another 24 hours to make an impact. Show up inside your life as someone who treats others better than expected, because it's the right thing to do, and not because you expect anything in return.

We all struggle at some point in our lives. The trap is thinking that no one understands. I'm here to tell you that is not the case. I understand, and I care. That's why I'm grateful for the adversity. That's why I pray with gratitude for the lessons. That's why I write and share my story—because I know what feeling alone is like. I know how it feels when you think you're the only one going through something.

Your life is impacting someone else's life. You're influencing someone. There is someone looking to you as a leader, and they are so grateful.

Grateful for my Village

"If you want to go fast, go alone. If you want to go far, go together." ~ African Proverb

Gratitude overwhelms me when thinking of those people who helped me in my journey. Not just the ones who sat in my chair, but the ones who held my hand, were a shoulder to cry on, stood by my side, or otherwise lent a hand. Those people are my village, my supporters, the people in my corner, and sometimes in my chair.

You probably have a lot of names for that group of people in your own life. Be grateful for them.

These are the people who help us do brave things. They help us do the things that scare us. I make sure that I'm scared at least once every day. And that's a good thing. When you're scared, you're doing something, you're learning and growing, and ultimately gaining new life experiences that will help others. That feeling gives me confidence that I'm on the right path.

If you're looking for the courage to be scared, look no further than gratitude. Stop and be grateful that you even have the opportunity. If you have a dream, and you're not scared of just going for it, you're not dreaming big enough. Gratitude ties your dream to vision and purpose.

That's when your heart starts pulling harder than your fear.

Do things that scare you. Use it as a guide to how you're living your life. If I haven't been scared for a few weeks, it's time to change something. When you're feeling scared, you're on the right path. Let that feeling pull you outside your comfort zone. It may sound strange but, being scared gives me courage and confidence. I'm actually grateful for fear. If I've learned anything on this journey, it's that this is not a dress rehearsal. Now is the best time of your life.

Every adversity life throws at you will challenge you. If you are brave and will be present through them, you will be profoundly changed. You will learn to go a bit deeper and be rewarded with amazing sunrises and sunsets, and they are that much sweeter when shared with those supporters, your village, who cheered you on.

Life is about being present and showing up for one another. Let's pick each other up when we fall. Let's celebrate each other and flip the narrative from "me" to "we." We are who we surround ourselves with. Make sure, beyond any doubt, that the people in your life know you love them. Tell them. Show them. Share love and kindness everywhere you go. Don't go to your grave with your song still in you. Sing.

Making an impact takes grit, determination, commitment, and hard work. It takes patience and persistence. It's a slow process that develops over time. Life is uncomfortable and messy.

Climbing that mountain to make great change means your hands will get dirty—but isn't that why they make soap?

Today is our day to celebrate the abundance in our lives. Celebrate your family and friends. What's so special about today? Is it a holiday? Maybe it is. Or maybe it's just another day to be thankful.

When you think about what you're thankful for today, consider and appreciate your abundant blessings, your choices, your village. This morning, I summed up my blessings in one word: life. I'm thankful for life. All of it.

I think the best way to be grateful is to live your best life.

FORGIVENESS

Forgiveness does not mean you erase the past or forget what has happened. It means you no longer use your feelings about it as poison against yourself.

With true forgiveness, you let go of the emotions around the person or event that keep you locked in a battle with the past.

This is something I know quite a bit about. There is no more brutally painful experience than forgiveness denied. It is as devastating to the one withholding forgiveness as the one being denied. Holding onto pain is foolish and damages everyone involved. Forgiving and letting go of feelings of resentment for one who has harmed you frees your heart to heal. There is nothing more powerful than forgiveness for healing deep wounds.

Denying forgiveness is like volunteering to serve a prison sentence for a crime committed by someone else. Forgiveness is extending grace to those who have caused you pain. I know how difficult it is to think of anything other than our own pain. But that is exactly what we must do.

Even harder is self-forgiveness. We all struggle to see past our physical and emotional imperfections to love ourselves. And that is the most important forgiveness there is.

Forgiving Myself

As a kid, I had no idea what I wanted to be when I grew up. Few did back then. We grew up watching our fathers and grandfathers. Some of us followed in their footsteps; some carved out new paths for themselves; others, like me, just wandered. For me, wandering was a sin. I had the best role model possible in my father and was surrounded by good people everywhere.

Success in whatever I chose to do was a no-brainer. But I was immature and selfish.

I chose to keep wandering. The first in a string of immature, selfish choices I would make. I wandered into a school I didn't want to attend, a marriage I could never sustain, a job I didn't like. I was lying to everyone, lying to myself, steeped in anger, using alcohol to dull the pain. The last immature, selfish choice was telling myself that as long as everything looked bright and shiny on the outside, the rest of it didn't matter.

I managed to convince myself that waking up every day broken and unfulfilled, with every personal relationship falling apart (marriage, children, parents), didn't matter.

When Terrilynn came into my life, there was light after years in total darkness. She showed me the path back to me. But she could not walk that path for me. I had to take that journey alone. Yes, she let me know it is OK to be vulnerable and taught me the meaning of accountability.

Left to make my own choices, I strayed off the path yet again. Thankfully, she did not abandon me. She stayed with me when she could have run away. She forgave me for hurting her and loved me toward forgiving myself.

I'm still judged on all those sins, let's face it, I was an easy target and did everything to earn it. I still carry them, but I have forgiven myself for the sins of my past. I have been overwhelming myself with guilt for years. It's not intentional;

well, maybe it is. Guilt is a powerful thing, it is a heavy load to carry in your heart, and it will overwhelm you if you allow it.

When you have caused harm to another, you will carry their pain with you. Nothing can numb it. The load just becomes heavier.

I've tried everything to shake it off:

- Denial—It wasn't my fault. Blame is always the easy path. A selfish Band-Aid that doesn't stop the bleeding.
- Rationalization—Making excuses, justifying, and explaining. Superficially valid in my mind, but not real in my heart. Adds insult to injury.
- Distraction—Throwing myself into work. Ignoring and refusing to acknowledge the pain. An extra burden.
- Truth—The right path. Real as a punch in the gut, raw as a skinned knee. But it still doesn't lighten the load.

I tried everything but forgiveness. Forgiveness allows you to let go of negative emotions. Brings you accountability. Forces you to take responsibility by treating the wound. Most importantly, it creates space for others to forgive you. For 20 years, I tried to become a better man. For 20 years, I carried the burden of guilt for negative behavior—"sins of the past," as they say. For 20 years, I couldn't move past it.

So I finally had to put it down.

If you can't move beyond the sins of the past, you will never experience an extraordinary life. Trust me on this one.

Doodles called me one day—there's Doodles in my chair again—and said, "Go to school." He said I needed to declutter my mindset and learn *why*. So, I started studying. The subject was me. I picked up my first journal, and I started to write. Then, I started to read. What I read was unexpected. I learned that when we know why, everything falls into place. When we don't, we must push things into place. And I've said many times from experience: you can't push that square peg into that round hole. Trust me on this one too.

After years of working hard to become a better man, and consistently tripping over my past, I learned that there is a big difference between working on something and working toward something. Now, I own every aspect of my life, the good and the bad. I know me emotionally, physically, and spiritually. I have forgiven myself for the sins of the past. I remember them, but I no longer trip over them because I have a life to live. Focus on making a difference, not on beating yourself up or feeling sorry for yourself. Focus on helping others, and you'll release the grip of guilt on your life.

If you've lost—and I have many times—you don't dwell on it. Forgive yourself for what happened, dig deeper, and commit to doing what is required to win the next time. The way you respond to losing determines success or failure. Every winner in life has lost.

You lost the game? Practice harder. You failed the exam? Study deeper. You didn't win the contract? Prepare to win the next one. You don't like where your life is going? Course-correct. Quit hanging onto those losses. Forgive and receive. Losing is not a boulder blocking your path to success; it's a stepping stone to success. What you see is what you believe in your heart to be true. If you believe you're a failure, you are. It's an inside job. Nobody can assign failure to you. You determine that. Forgive yourself. It's not worth keeping yourself down.

There is not one single perfect human being walking this earth. We are all perfectly imperfect. Forgive yourself quickly. Give yourself love and grace. Be patient when you are wrong and compassionate when you stumble and fall. Do not place conditions on your life.

Self-forgiveness lights your life. It becomes the ever-vigilant beacon that shines from your heart. It shows everyone that you have healed and draws all who see it to your story.

Forgiving Others

Within it, forgiveness carries vulnerability, faith, acceptance, accountability, and gratitude.

God puts people in our lives for a reason. Good and bad, each one is a blessing. That's the truth. Think of the most negative, miserable person you've ever met, the person who has tried or has done you harm, and thank God for making that happen. I've learned so much from every negative person that has been in my life that I wouldn't change those experiences. In fact, I even wish those well who have caused me harm. They have made me strong and resilient. I've grown exponentially as a man because of them. I won't allow anyone to make me hate them. That's just not something I let into my life.

When you hate, hold grudges, and fill your heart with anger and fear, you only take away your own power and energy. That's wasted energy you could be focusing on transforming your life.

The reason I can write and speak truthfully and openly from my heart is because I am able to let go and forgive others. I have been the subject of damaging rumors, spread by people I thought were friends. I was angry, until I realized my anger was only hurting me. So I forgave them, and to my surprise, I discovered that they were still my friends. We all make mistakes. We all have been hurt and hurt others. We are all human. I won't waste a second of my precious time hating anyone. I have too much living to do.

Circumstances are never beyond your control. You're always a choice away—at least, in how you respond to situations. We can choose how we respond to any circumstance, even when something bad happens. That choice we make in the moment defines what comes next.

Ultimately, you are not a product of your circumstances; you're a product of your choices.

So how do we choose to react to those who hurt us? We also need to ask, "Is it possible to love everyone?" Considering that there are many levels of love, I think it is. We are all human and subject to our bad choices, imperfections, and weaknesses. We can love everyone if we can accept, forgive, and be kind to all. Isn't that what love is? Love contains empathy and compassion.

I think compassion for our fellow humans is important, but empathy is the most critical part of love. Empathy comes from putting yourself in someone else's shoes and seeing things from their perspective. I know it's possible to connect with everyone with meaning and depth.

All that's needed are an open heart and an open mind.

Truth, Courage, and ... Forgiveness

"Vulnerability sounds like truth and feels like courage."
~ Brené Brown

Have you ever felt lost, rejected, or betrayed?

Sadly, I have. In the short term, it is devastatingly painful. But, over time, the pain fades, and you find the courage to trust and move on. You feel vulnerable, struggling to trust, and you're not sure if you can ever forgive. Don't close the door on your life; rather open it, and let love in. Open your heart and reach out to another.

The only way to be loved is to love. The only way to be trusted is to trust.

Have you ever caused another to feel lost, rejected, or betrayed? Hopefully unintentionally. You likely know what that feels like as well. Sadly, I do. In the short term, there is no pain. But, over time you become aware of the pain, and the effects are devastating. You feel vulnerable, struggling to be trusted, and not sure if you'll ever be forgiven.

Don't close the door on your life; rather open it, and let love in. Open your heart and reach out to another.

Oceans are a mirror of human life. At once beautifully calm and serene, yet always possessing devastatingly destructive power. Relentless waves of its own creation always moving with the current ... crests and troughs.

Like the ocean's waves, our lives are our own creations. We move with the current of time, always seeking a distant shore. We have crests that give us courage, and troughs that make us vulnerable. Somewhere in between lives trust and forgiveness. We sometimes get so caught up in our own lives that we forget that other people exist, and that other people are holding onto expectations of us that we may not realize.

If you have caused someone harm, don't drag that burden around the rest of your life ... be accountable. Have the courage to ask for forgiveness.

Anger is a wasted emotion. Life is too short to be angry; it just clouds your judgment. It is truly the coward's path. We all experience difficult moments in life, where we want to give up. It's called being human. In those moments, anger was my default setting. You can imagine ... that didn't go well.

I still have difficult moments where I want to give up. Now I'm honest in those moments. I think of the person I want to be, and I act in accordance with that. Anger is no longer an option.

The person I consider myself to be does these five things *always*:

- Always be willing to lead.
- Always be willing to fail.
- Always be kind.
- Always control your emotions.
- Always choose gratitude.

If you find yourself having one of those moments, or you're in a place you don't prefer, refer to those five things to guide you. It works. Alignment of mind, body, and spirit happens when your default is founded upon a predetermined set of positive thoughts, beliefs, and actions.

Anger vanishes, fear dissipates, confidence soars, and gratitude takes control. The result is happiness, love, fulfillment, and peace.

Sometimes, the hardest lessons are the most valuable. Choose each day to be present in the beautiful moments between the moments. Have fun, get out of your comfort zone, and share the love. Learn from others, soak up wisdom, and prepare for the future. Live your life consciously, aware that each moment you breathe is a gift. And let go of the anger. It doesn't serve you in the present.

LIGHTHOUSE

You probably remember the parable of the tugboat and the lighthouse that I talked about earlier in this book.

They save ships in drastically different ways. The tugboat goes out to push and pull an individual boat, expending an enormous amount of energy and effort to get itself and the single ship to safety, while the lighthouse simply stands, fixed, and shines its bright light.

Let's get real for a moment. I have lived in fear of judgment, been tortured by lies of betrayal, suffered loss of a loved one, and endured bankruptcy. That is some heavy stuff, and it represents the darkest times of my life. Because of these things, I've missed out on life at times, paralyzed by fear, realizing that being the betrayer is worse than being betrayed, losing my father, and the bankruptcy of my moral and financial bank accounts.

Some painful moments, some embarrassing moments ... all difficult to own. But accountability comes easy when believing. Sharing comes confidently when believing. Regret comes surely, but quietly when framed with a story of coming back. I'm back, though the memories still linger. I'm healed, though the scars are a constant reminder.

I'm burdened, though the load I carry is lighter. I'm dark, though the road ahead is brighter.

I spent too many years as a tugboat, putting out too much energy for the wrong people and for the wrong reasons, accomplishing only to fail myself and the people closest to me.

Have you felt empty? I did ... empty, hollow, or incomplete, whatever you want to call it.

Let's go with "incomplete." I was serving on nonprofit boards, volunteering in my community, and giving back whenever I could.

My heart was full, but even though I couldn't see what was missing, I knew there was more.

I didn't like that feeling. Naturally, I started searching, frantically at times, for someone, something to complete me. It was futile of course. Resentment mounted with each disappointment, which led to chronic frustration and running on empty. One day, I got tired of feeling incomplete. That day, I made a commitment to telling and listening to the truth. The truth was that the missing piece wasn't out there, in fact, it wasn't missing at all.

Suddenly, the tank was no longer empty.

Did I find it ... that elusive and magical key to peace, love, and happiness? Nope. I didn't find it. The truth is, there is no key, no formula, no magic dust. You already have everything you need—a heart that feels and a soul that knows. You only need to convince your mind to listen. That day I told myself the truth, I didn't set a goal, I made a commitment to loving and trusting myself and living to my full potential. I made a commitment to becoming a better man.

So, if you are ever feeling empty, or like me, incomplete, don't be afraid to listen to the truth within you. It will set you free. Now I am a lighthouse. I stand firm and radiate my light to help as many people as I can by sharing things that are positive to help others.

There are people who come into your life to shine a light on the human spirit and what you can accomplish no matter what life throws at you. They teach you to believe in yourself so your spirit will soar above any adversity. We humans can transform or destroy lives—our own and those in our wake.

Every one of us will be challenged in our lifetime; no one is immune from adversity. We don't have to surrender. We can believe and use adversity to propel us to soar to unimaginable heights.

We're defined by the movement in our minds, our imaginations. Where that mindset movement leads our hearts creates purpose and builds meaning into our lives. Purpose and meaning are connected to our well-being. Life is a beautiful experience, meant to be shared. That helps give us purpose. It takes courage to be positive and share our lives with others.

It's not always sunshine and rainbows. But, without the bad, we wouldn't understand or appreciate the good. There can't be light without dark; it's the balance of the universe.

So, until I sat in the dark and felt it, there was no light. It's within our darkest moments that we find the most profound truth.

What I found was the light within, the light that's inside all of us. We can run from the dark or embrace it and let the light shine through. It's a choice. Maybe our lives must be stripped bare for us to truly see ourselves. Maybe then we can shine our light and help other people shine a little brighter as well. When you have been healed and ultimately saved by the light of another, your purpose will be clearly defined.

The Darkness of Lies

I've allowed space in my life to keep me from having the kind of relationship with my children that I wanted, a space filled with lies, excuses, and fear. A space drawn by my own hand. I love them and miss them every day. Yet, I can say that in this moment right now, if this is the best it ever gets, then I will be living a happy life.

My father said to me after one of my monumental screw-ups, "The purpose of life is to live a life of purpose." Like always, he gave me just enough to start digging for more. What I ultimately got from that was, "All things are possible until you convince yourself otherwise." When you believe, everything is at your fingertips.

Purpose and meaning come to you and flow through you.

There was a time when I was incapable of original thought, or it appears, telling the truth. All creativity within my heart and mind was buried beneath a mountain of self-pity. Depression hung over me like a vulture waiting for me to surrender.

When I finally bled enough and got help, the most amazing thing happened. I found my compass.

At some point in our lives, we all stray off the beaten path. I didn't find my compass until turned inward, toward my center—the place where the light is—and found what is real inside me. Then, I began to understand the deep thoughts and feelings that I had been suppressing. It occurred to me that there may be others out there in a similar place—perhaps others who were staring into the abyss that I had just climbed out of.

It was then that I decided to share my thoughts.

I have always been a great speaker. The problem is I did not always speak the truth. The power of our words does not come from our own eloquence, spirited delivery, or from quoting something that someone famous said.

Powerful words are rarely clever or witty; they are just honest. Their power comes from simply speaking the truth within the deepest recesses of our burning souls and expressing that truth in our own words. There is a place inside all of us where that pure truth lives.

The truth is ... the thing holding you back is a lack of self-awareness.

Let's face it: failing is painful. But if we had never been told that, what amazing things would we willingly try? What important lessons would we openly seek and learn? Most of us don't want to fail because we're more worried about how others view that failure than about seeing the lesson on the other side of it. Seek approval from one person and one person only: YOU.

Get out of your own way. Failure is temporary, learn from it, and move past it quickly. Learn how to fail forward. If you're going to create the life you want, you'll need to get uncomfortable, sacrifice, and be willing to fail—publicly if necessary—to become the best you can be.

I've been there, afraid to fail.

I've had situations that ripped me wide open. And that fear made me the poster boy of underachieving.

Then I was reminded a few years ago that I wasn't living to the full potential of the gifts given to me. I had dimmed my light when I should have been a lighthouse for others. I knew it was inside me, and I intentionally kept it there. Never, ever dim your light for anyone or anything. Be the lighthouse. Shine brightly through the storm. Step into your most powerful and unapologetic self. Be the first to go into the unknown and shine brightly. Go forward along your journey with respect, enthusiasm, humility, and truth.

In that space, you'll develop the positive mindset required to build your foundation of success.

The Light Lies in Authenticity

There is freedom in authenticity. But people will always try to advise us, persuade us, analyze us, and judge us, making the truth elusive.

Everyone has portrayed themselves to be someone or something we are not. Maybe this means trying to impress a girl that may be just a bit out of our league or getting a raise that maybe we don't deserve. The truth is that none of us is completely truthful all the time. Especially to ourselves. We must accept and embrace our inner truth, even if we don't like what it says about us.

But we can't just speak the truth—there's more to it than that. We must live it. We must be who we say we are and do what we say we will do.

How do we become authentically true to ourselves? The first step is to not be concerned with being "right." When we understand that it is more important to be real and honest than right, we have found our compass and are going in the right direction. The next step is to be passionate and courageous, the key ingredients necessary to become a truthful person.

All the noise of the world around us can cause confusion and dilute the truth. With all the distraction, it is difficult to hear our inner voice speaking our own unique truth.

Speak your truth, share your thoughts and feelings, and you'll develop confidence and virtually eliminate self-doubt from your life. Our truth is worth fighting for because the words you speak become the house in which you live. It might as well be a lighthouse.

My purpose is to be like a lighthouse, shining my light on the shadows so others can avoid the adversity that I have encountered. In the darkest time of my life, the soft illumination from a lighthouse within one loving heart saved my wayward soul.

Every experience in our lives contributes to shaping us into who we are. Live. Love. Learn. Pray. Inspire. is the solid foundation upon which your lighthouse can shine brightly, a trusted beacon providing hope and guiding wayward souls that come within range of its brilliant beam of light.

Be Weird

My first and perhaps most important professional mentor, Bruce Fletcher, first sat in my chair when he hired me for the job that ultimately would give me the platform to fulfill my purpose and vision of my life. He certainly was unconventional in his methods, but he built my confidence by believing in me and guiding me through the most difficult period in my life. He was the only one who was willing to tell me the truth about myself during a time when I was trying as hard as I could to avoid hearing it.

Leadership is not a one-size-fits-all thing. Bruce is not what anyone would call a visionary leader. In fact, Bruce is just ... well, he's just weird. He totally owns his weirdness. That is what makes him an exceptional leader and mentor.

Those that do not know him will not see his genius through all his happy-go-lucky silliness. Bruce is a leader who mentors and teaches his lessons freely and will even throw in the occasional pop quiz. Just to see if you have been paying attention, he will put you in harm's way, gauge your reaction then pull you back at the last possible moment. The fact that he is extremely entertained by this should have no bearing on your opinion of his leadership skills. I told you he is weird. Perhaps Bruce's greatest trait, the one thing that sets him apart and makes him effective as a leader and mentor is his loyalty.

Motives aside, he will do anything to help you succeed.

Like Bruce, I have always been the square peg in a round hole. The problem for me was that I didn't own my weirdness, my truth. Then not fitting in turned into fighting to fit in. Once I stopped wanting to fit in, I did. And I was miserable. Now I have finally ended the battle. Now I own my weirdness. I embrace my quirks, flaws, my "different"—in fact, different is one of my favorite words and the biggest compliment anyone could ever give me. I strive to be different.

Just before he died, my father told me, "Be the lighthouse. Lead the way, and leave no one behind."

When you are the lighthouse, you will see the beauty around you, your critics will become scarce, and your blessings will become abundant. Be weird. Your people, the right people, will be attracted to your light.

I have learned over the years to love my uniqueness. It's our unique weirdness that makes us beautiful. Please, please lift your unique voice. A world in turmoil needs to hear it. In owning your unique weirdness, you become a voice, a beacon of peace and harmony.

Until the voice of peace is audible above the din, we will continue to lose ourselves.

As for Bruce and me, we will be out there being lighthouses for the misfits and rebels of the world, sharing our weirdness and leading the way forward. We know there are others, and they are the same "different" as us. When all the misfits and rebels in the world come together with one powerful, uplifting voice, amazing things will happen. We will learn to accept each other. We will begin to respect each other. We will simply love each other for who we are as uniquely weird human beings.

Live out loud and be original so you stand out in the sea of sameness, and you will find your tribe. There, you will fit in.

My existence on this planet, at this moment, is not random. I didn't just fall from the sky. I was chosen to be here. I was given this life for a reason. I'm my own light.

When I was 16, on a vacation to Hilton Head, Doodles made me climb a lighthouse just to tell me this, "A lighthouse doesn't just shine its light to see if passing ships are paying attention. It illuminates the dangerous shoreline to keep them from harm's way." When I was probably 46, I finally understood what he meant: It's better to Illuminate than to merely shine. Do something that will have a profound impact on future generations.

The Person in the Chair

Be truth's voice, illuminate the real leaders who serve, and drown out the voice of the pretenders. Our children are watching. Our grandchildren are waiting. Do something that will not only change your life but will change their world.

SITTING IN YOUR CHAIR

Many years have passed since I began my journey inward. There have been many mistakes along the way. My body has gotten older, my mind wiser, but regardless of what the calendar tells me, my illuminated heart and soaring spirit tell me I am younger than that now.

The Five Pillars have become my mission. The chapters in this book represent the significant milestones along this most daring adventure to find myself. I have learned the importance of vulnerability, the immense beauty of accountability, and the life-changing power of forgiveness, just some of the pieces that support the Five Pillars.

Every ending represents a new beginning. We are privileged to travel our own unique path through life. Mine has seen challenges that, at times, proved overwhelming and mistakes that brought devastating consequences. The mistakes made in my first marriage led to the most devastating failure of my life and interrupted my journey in a way that would change me forever. There have been lessons. The scrapes and bruises have healed, but a few scars remain. I didn't plan them, but I can learn from them.

You simply cannot plan your life. Sooner or later, you must jump into the deep end of the pool. Now I'm closer to 70 than I am to 40, one of the few regrets I have is that I didn't jump in sooner.

I've learned a couple of things that you should know:

1. The "perfect life" doesn't exist.

We tend to look at others in comparison ... celebrities, athletes, entrepreneurs ... to try cobbling together the perfect life rather than looking in the mirror. The truth is the only perfect life is the one you're living.

2. You have an expiration date.

Every one of us was born with an expiration date, yet most of us go about our days as if we'll live forever. We get caught in the mundane routine and forget to live while we're alive. Go all-in while you're here—there's literally nothing to lose.

3. Everything matters.

Every moment, every smile, every handshake, every conversation, every person, every decision, every opportunity, every kiss ... everything matters. You don't want to miss anything. Stop talking. Start doing. Get out there and write your story. You have everything you need. Because when it's all said and done, you'll be more thankful you made that jump than you could ever imagine. And when you're 70, you won't be the guy talking about what could have been.

Life is about connection. We're all connected to the earth and to each other. You can never truly know the impact you are having on the planet. We know it's critically important to take care in how we physically impact our planet, we're destroying the only home we have, but taking care in how we impact our fellow humans is equally important. Every day, your actions impact someone.

Talking to a friend of mine who is in his 70s, I realized how fragile life truly is. If I'm blessed to live to be 84 like my father, that gives me less than 10,000 days left. I'm not going to waste a single one. There is so much work to do in those remaining days

... and so much living. Realizing it will end allows an incredible depth of lightness and love into your life. Live the life you're called to live. Pursue your purpose as if your life depends on it. Be grateful for the lessons of the past, and share what you learned from them. Believe in you, believe in me, believe in humanity, and share your heart and soul freely. You will ignite a passion and enthusiasm that will echo through every aspect of your life.

The lessons I've learned along the way have forged a better man. He is accountable for those choices. He is someone who loves deeply. He is someone who forgives quickly. He is someone who cares openly. He is someone who believes faithfully. He is someone who wants the best for all people.

He is someone who rose above every hardship because, even in his darkest hours, he still showed up.

In 1910 President Theodore Roosevelt, my favorite American president (I think Teddy would have been a cool dude to hang out with) gave a speech called "Citizenship in a Republic" at the Sorbonne in Paris. Here is an excerpt that I consider the most important part of that speech: "If he fails, at least he fails while daring greatly, so that his place shall never be with those cold and timid souls who neither know victory nor defeat."

That line inspires me, and I hope it inspires you too. Always dare greatly and fail greatly in the direction of doing good. Never allow anyone to change you ... only *you* decide when and why change is necessary. Never, ever quit ... because the next time you stumble, it may be success itself extending a hand to help you stand up.

You're the only one standing in your way.

Build Your Pillars

I read something recently that is so simple and yet so very profound: "If your presence doesn't make an impact, your absence won't make a difference."

Legacy isn't flashy or sexy. Legacy is gritty, covered in sweat, maybe a drop or two of blood ... and certainly more tears than can be captured. Legacy is, above all else, impactful. I remind myself all the time that this is what matters. It isn't about "me." It's about the Five Pillars and sharing this message.

Live:

Nothing in life is more important than your health. Your life is happening right now, and you have a responsibility to live it well. Exercise your mind, body, and spirit. Read every day to keep your mind clear. Move your body every day ... push/pull/rotate. Pray every day to keep your faith strong.

Love:

Love is everything. There is extraordinary power in loving all people. And your first love should be you. Learn to appreciate who you are, and you will freely appreciate the unique gifts of the man and woman next to you. Nothing is possible in life without love.

Learn:

Know what you don't know. Learn from the harvest of those planters who went before you and plant your seeds so others following you may reap a harvest of their own. Some amazing people provided me with the seeds that I would plant along my journey through life. Nurture them so they grow strong. If they don't ...

Remember it's not the seed; it's the farmer.

Pray:

When I was a kid, I said my prayers every night before going to bed. Then I grew up and began to pray a little less, pushing my faith a little deeper in my heart. After all, I knew everything. Then life happened, and the clouds rolled in. I started making mistakes and bad decisions. Then I became a little older, maybe wiser, and with few other options, I began to pray a little. The storm clouds lifted, and the sun reappeared. My faith was pushed back to the surface.

You don't need to wait for the dark times to pray; God listens when it's sunny, too.

Inspire:

You never know who is watching or the impact you are having on someone's life. You never know who you are inspiring. People who inspire aren't always the ones on stage shouting and offering their $99 "Roadmap to Success." The most inspiring people are usually ordinary people stepping up and doing extraordinary things.

Let's not forget why we exist. Let's not forget what our purpose is here. This isn't about money. This isn't about recognition. We are here to make a difference in this world ... and we are doing it. We are changing. We are growing. We are evolving. We are improving and strengthening our community and adding momentum to our mission.

So, let's do this. Share your thoughts, your words, and your time to improve lives and change our world.

The Power of Why

One of my favorite passages in the Bible says, "We rejoice in our sufferings, knowing that suffering produces endurance, and endurance produces character, and character produces hope." (Romans 5:3-5)

We become who we are because of our journey, our experiences, our scars. They define us.

Compared to all the other ways we are defined, by our family and friends, colleagues, and total strangers, our definition of ourselves is unique. And it's the only one that matters. Because I believe in who I am and why I'm here, I show up every day. Now, even the days where I take the occasional punch in the gut (yes that still happens) don't knock me down anymore.

I see the beauty in life, even in the punches. Once you believe in yourself, how you define yourself will not change, even when you do. It will remain constant through all seasons of your life because your purpose is fixed.

We, being the crazy, optimistic, dreamers in my world, believe that, by changing the way people think, we can change the world. Maybe that's naïve, but I happen to be an idealistic child of the 1960s, and being a bit naïve is probably a good thing in today's world.

Making a child smile, feeding someone who's hungry, or saving a life by donating your blood ... there is a way everyone can help someone. In 20 years, people won't remember what clothes you wore, which car you drove, and maybe not even your full name. They will remember the mark you left on the world.

Sit in someone's chair, welcome others into yours, listen, learn, and be the Five Pillars. Keep them in your heart and be the leader you were meant to be.

TAKE ACTION

The words Live, Love, Learn, Pray, and Inspire are beautiful when spoken, but it's the action they inspire that makes them powerful. How you implement these words in your life is entirely within your control. Your life is a journey to yourself. It isn't about when your journey begins, it's about the living you have done along the way. Because it's the act of living that makes you alive. It's in that action that the right people find their way into your chair ... exactly when you need them.

I found hope for the person I was by moving toward the person I could become.

The only obstacle I faced on my journey was my own lack of action. Mine has been a long and, at times, painful journey. I would take three steps forward, then two steps back. If not for the people in my chair, my journey would have ended far too early. A piece of every one of them lives in my heart. They have cultivated a seed in my soul that has changed me. I feel their presence in everything I do.

What I know about life has been taught by them, and the path to what I know about myself has been inspired by them. Because of the light they have shined on the core of my being, I will continue seeking what I don't know. At your core, you know. That's the place deep inside you where your heart and soul unite and become your core. There you know who you are. You only need to be brave enough to embrace your truth and become whatever that is...and that takes a village.

Don't waste a minute of your precious time. Get to your core and embrace the truth you find waiting there. There's nothing to be afraid of, you're already here. Being born was the hard part. That day you were blessed with your chair for a reason, not to sit in it and wait for your life to find you, or to force someone that you envy to occupy it so you can live their life as yours.

No, that blessing of the empty chair requires you to be an active participant in your journey.

Everything happens for a reason. An experience that one person takes for granted can be life-changing for another. We're placed in situations we may not understand, but we have to accept that it's the right time, at the right place, with the right people to learn something we need to know. The people who sit in your chair are there to teach you and guide you on your journey through life, not live your life for you. You can't just watch your life pass you by. We're just a piece of something bigger and we need the pieces of all the people who sit in our chair along this journey to make us whole.

What does Live, Love, Learn, Pray, and Inspire look like in action?

Live means to embrace every new day with gratitude for another opportunity to do better and be better, to be kind and gentle with yourself and others.

Love means loving yourself as you are with no filters ... and to seek out and love those who are unlovable without conditions. *Learn* is about opening your heart and mind to all the wonders of life, especially the ones your eyes can't see, and knowing that what you don't know is far more important than what you do.

Pray is about having faith in your quiet moments to align your physical, emotional, and spiritual worlds, and to continue walking forward when all seems lost.

Inspire is to lead by example, as the person you are meant to be ... raw and unfiltered, and infused with love, grace, patience, and compassion.

That's your call to action. That's how you step from the dark into the light. Sharing the love with every life you encounter. Giving grace to those who are wrong. Being patient with the critics and embracing a future you can't see with faith. Showing compassion for those who have stumbled in your path. Speaking these beautiful and encouraging words from your heart to nourish and inspire others.

And receiving these blessings ten-fold in return.

ABOUT THE AUTHOR

My name is James Protin. My professional journey spans 40 years in the engineering and construction industry. Did I mention that I'm not an engineer? It quickly became apparent that I would never be the smartest person in the room, so I had no choice but to become the hardest worker in every room I would enter.

This worked for a time, and I was able to push through my twenties. Then my life went off the rails. Darkness came, and I became an imposter. Words like anxiety, codependency, people-pleasing, and trauma dominated my story. At 35, I was being dismantled by depression. At 40, I thought my life was over, I was stuck, struggling to tread water. So, naturally, I burned it all to the ground. At 45, I started the journey to me. By 50, I started to recognize myself, and those words were replaced with new ones like gratitude, humility, empathy, and forgiveness. At 64, I know my life is just beginning.

My knowledge regarding mental health and emotional well-being wasn't learned from a textbook. I earned it by working myself away from a past marred by depression.

Looking back on my journey, there's nothing linear about it. The peaks and valleys and the multiple detours have all served a purpose. If I could go back in the day and change something, the only thing I would change would be my time in my twenties. I would invest more in figuring out who I really was.

I tried therapy and flunked out. I failed miserably. Then a mentor suggested I start journaling as a substitute for traditional therapy ... and it's been one of the best things I've ever done. I discovered that I love writing, so much so, that I am writing a book that will publish in 2023. It's amazing how, when you stare at a blank page and spill your heart all over it, all the feels, especially the ones you don't like to show people, you unlock everything. What appears on the page is brutally honest, sometimes painful, and always enlightening.

Navigating transformation is never easy. Each of us is taking a journey that is uniquely ours. But when you share your true story, you will help someone who is struggling along their own. That's where Live, Love, Learn, Pray, and Inspire come in. To inspire change, you must tell the hard truths. In that space, we see how our experiences can benefit others. There is a strength that rises from my story, and allows me to carry everyone I've ever met in my heart, and together we will positively impact every life we encounter.

ABOUT THE JAMES PROTIN PODCAST

James started journaling as a form of therapy and discovered a passion for writing. He has written a daily blog since 2012. With the blog building a loyal following, and at the suggestion of a long-time mentor, James, and producer/videographer Nick Altland launched the James Protin Podcast in March of 2022. Every week, he shares the experiences that have defined his journey and talks with people who have their own powerful stories to tell. With this podcast, you will witness stories of love, faith, gratitude, forgiveness, and redemption. The conversations will be unfiltered, filled with thought-provoking questions and hopefully a few answers.

Guests will discuss facing fear and overcoming adversity to succeed in business, leadership, entrepreneurship, education, relationships, and more. The conversations promise to be raw and gritty ... and will always be entertaining. Just like real life. Live. Love. Learn. Pray. and Inspire. is about feeling everything and living life to its fullest. Along with his guests, the podcast seeks to inspire, engage, and create impactful dialogue. That's the essence of the podcast. It's about doing better and being better in life, business, and all things in between.

The blog, podcast, and book are based on the five pillars of leadership that James's father taught him by "sitting in his chair"—by taking the time to advise and inspire because it mattered.

Listen to the podcast at https://www.youtube.com/@thejamesprotinpodcast.